CUTTING-EDGE band saw tips & tricks

CUTTING-EDGE
band saw
tips & tricks

*How to get the most
out of your band saw*

KENNETH BURTON

POPULAR
WOODWORKING
BOOKS

CINCINNATI, OHIO
www.popularwoodworking.com

Cutting-Edge Band Saw Tips & Tricks. Copyright © 2004 by Kenneth Burton. Printed and bound in the China. All rights reserved. No part of this book may be reproduced in any form or by any electronic or mechanical means, including information storage and retrieval systems, without permission in writing from the publisher, except by a reviewer, who may quote brief passages in a review. Published by Popular Woodworking Books, an imprint of F+W Publications, Inc., 4700 East Galbraith Road, Cincinnati, Ohio, 45236. First edition.

Visit our Web site at www.popularwoodworking.com for information on more resources for woodworkers.

Other fine Popular Woodworking Books are available from your local bookstore or direct from the publisher.

08   07   06   05   04   5   4   3   2   1

Library of Congress Cataloging-in-Publication Data

Burton, Kenneth S.
    Cutting-edge band saw tips & tricks: how to get the most out of your band saw / Kenneth Burton.
        p.   cm.
    Includes index.
    ISBN 1-55870-702-6 (paperback: alk. paper)
    ISBN 1-55870-741-7 (hardcover: alk. paper)
    1. Band saws.   2. Woodwork.   I. Title: Band saw tips & tricks.   II. Title.
TT186.B83   2004   200404103
684'.083--dc22   CIP

Acquisitions editor: Jim Stack
Editor: Amy Hattersley
Designer: Brian Roeth
Layout artist: Joni DeLuca
Production coordinator: Robin Richie
Technical illustrator: Melanie Powell

READ THIS IMPORTANT SAFETY NOTICE

METRIC CONVERSION CHART

to convert	to	multiply by
Inches	Centimeters	2.54
Centimeters	Inches	0.4
Feet	Centimeters	30.5
Centimeters	Feet	0.03
Yards	Meters	0.9
Meters	Yards	1.1
Sq. Inches	Sq. Centimeters	6.45
Sq. Centimeters	Sq. Inches	0.16
Sq. Feet	Sq. Meters	0.09
Sq. Meters	Sq. Feet	10.8
Sq. Yards	Sq. Meters	0.8
Sq. Meters	Sq. Yards	1.2
Pounds	Kilograms	0.45
Kilograms	Pounds	2.2
Ounces	Grams	28.4
Grams	Ounces	0.035

For Emma Janelle, who really needs another book to chew on.

About the Author

Ken Burton has been working with wood professionally for the past 22 years. He holds a bachelor of science degree in industrial arts education from Millersville University of Pennsylvania and a master of fine arts degree from the School for American Crafts at the Rochester Institute of Technology.

Currently Burton operates Windy Ridge Woodworks in New Tripoli, Pennsylvania, where he designs and builds studio furniture and custom cabinetry and teaches woodworking workshops. His latest endeavor is to set up a blacksmithing forge (far away from the sawdust). He also teaches at the Yestermorrow Design/Build School in Warren, Vermont, and at the Peters Valley Craft Education Center in Layton, New Jersey.

During the school year, Burton is department leader for the Technology Education at Boyertown Area Senior High School.

Married to Susan and father to Sarah and Emma, Burton has turned to writing to get a word in edgewise. You can contact him at ksburton@fast.net.

Acknowledgements

A book such as this one involves many people in both direct and indirect ways. I couldn't have done it without the support and help of my family. So thank you, Sarah and Emma, who put up with their grumpy father for far too many long nights, and especially to Susan, who did way more than her share of parenting, housekeeping and everything else while this book was percolating.

Thanks, too, to my photography team: Jared Haas and Jeff Day. You guys may have the best hands in the business. Your patience and encouragement with my amateur photography skills were much appreciated.

Thanks as well to the many folks who were kind enough to contribute tools and expertise to this endeavor, including Kendell Smith at Delta Tools, Ed Scent at Highland Hardware, Louis Iturra at Iturra Design, Henry Wang at Micro Jig, David Hatton at Hoyle Products and Cheryl Hopkins at Ryobi Power Tools and special thanks to Don McClure for cutting down and supplying me with the logs I used in the lumbermaking section.

And finally to the crew at Popular Woodworking Books, including editors Jim Stack and Amy Hattersley, designer Brian Roeth and production coordinator Robin Richie. Thank you for allowing me to write this book and for putting together such a good-looking product.

table of contents

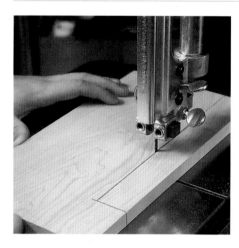

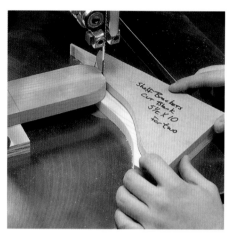

[PROJECTS]

introduction

After I had about worn out my Dremel scroll saw, my father finally relented and showed me how to use his band saw. I was 12 or 13 years old at the time. I remember how exciting it was to be able to flip a switch and easily make cuts that were barely possible on my beloved Dremel. Life hasn't been the same since.

That first band saw was a dominant presence in Dad's shop. It sat to the left of the entry and was the first thing you saw as you entered the room. This 18" model from the Gilliom Manufacturing Company was built from plywood with aluminum castings. It was noisy and throbbed as it ran. But it sure could cut. By the time I moved out, I had used it to cut everything from cabriole legs to $\frac{1}{8}$" strips for bent laminations.

Having access to that saw – and eventually the rest of the shop – led to a career working with wood and showing others how to do it. I currently teach in a classroom equipped with four band saws. They're among the first power tools I allow my eighth-graders to use. It is fun to watch as these kids learn to cut wood. Some take to the saw with immediate confidence, while others approach with fear and trepidation. Usually, however, by the time they leave my room for the last time, most of them use the saws without a second thought. What they don't realize, however, is that they have only scratched the surface of what a band saw can do.

What I have discovered in the workshops I teach in my own studio is that many woodworkers aren't really sure what a band saw can do, either. Many of them think the saw is pretty good at cutting curves, but beyond that, things get a little fuzzy. The truth is, the band saw is incredibly versatile. Sure, it can cut curves, but that's just the beginning. With the right blade and a careful tune-up, the band saw can cut precision joinery, make wafer-thin veneers, saw lumber from logs, even sculpt elegant boxes.

I put this book together to show woodworkers how to do all these things and more. The techniques presented here are those I use in my own shop, so I know they work. And the jigs and fixtures I've included are those that I have developed to overcome problems and accomplish more in an efficient, accurate manner. I encourage you to try them, modify them and adapt them to your own way of working. If you come up with any improvements, please let me know. I am always ready to try out new techniques.

A word of warning: This book is not intended as a buying guide to band saws or band saw accessories. I've included a few things you can buy, and I discuss some of the features to look for in a saw, but my main intent was to put forth a book full of ideas you could use with any saw. If you're in the market for a band saw, I suggest you consult *Popular Woodworking* magazine or one of the other periodicals that do tool reviews. These publications are in a much better position to give you the most up-to-date information in a fair and unbiased manner.

Also, keep in mind that while the band saw is one of the safer power tools, it can still bite. The techniques I have included here are all shop-tested and safe, but they are not totally risk free. If something doesn't seem right to you, or makes you hesitate, don't do it. Consult someone who is familiar with the technique, or try to find some other way around it. Better yet, come and take one of my classes; we welcome woodworkers of all experience levels.

By the way, Dad recently sold that old plywood saw and replaced it with one of the benchtop models. The smaller saw is more appropriate for grandchildren to use, or so he claims. The last I heard of the old saw, it was still going strong and was being used to make garden silhouettes – granny fannies and the like. Perhaps not the finest of woodwork, but I'm glad to know it is still being used.

I hope you enjoy the book and find new ways to put your band saw to use.

Ken Burton
Windy Ridge Woodworks

making straight cuts

LIKE MOST WOODWORKING machines, the band saw is a pretty simple affair. Most machines have two wheels that the blade runs around and a table to support your work as you cut. Along with a few assorted guards to keep the OSHA (Occupational Safety and Health Administration) folks happy, and a motor to supply power, that's about all there is to a band saw.

The size of a band saw is determined by the diameter of its wheels: A 14" saw has 14"-diameter wheels. This, in turn, governs the size of the piece that will fit between the blade and the column (the vertical riser that supports the upper wheel). To some extent, this limits the size of the pieces you can cut. Keep in mind, however, that as there is no column to the right of the blade, you can cut just about any size piece as long as the cutoff fits to the left of the blade. The other limiting factor is the distance from the table to the underside of the blade guard. This determines the maximum thickness of the pieces you can cut.

As with most purchases, choosing a band saw depends on a series of compromises. You need to balance the amount of space you have to devote to a band saw against the size of the pieces you intend to cut against the depth of your pockets. The small 9" saw shown in the photo is a great choice for a small shop. It is reasonably priced and will cut stock up to about 1" thick with ease. It can cut thicker material, but if you intend to cut a lot of heavy stock, you are going to want a saw with a little more power.

The medium-size saw in the photo is a 14" model equipped with an accessory riser block. This is perhaps the most common band saw in small shops across the country. Fourteen-inch saws typically have motors in the $\frac{3}{4}$ to $1\frac{1}{2}$ horsepower range. If you intend to use your saw for resawing wide boards, a more powerful motor is worth the extra money. In all likelihood, a 14" saw will handle most of your woodworking needs and still plug into a regular, household receptacle.

The final machine in the photo is an older 20" model. Larger industrial machines such as this can be a joy to use with their increased capacities, high-powered motors and heavy, vibration-damping castings. But they are also backbreaking to move, are bulky and often require heavy-duty electrical wiring. They are also quite a bit more expensive than their smaller counterparts.

Note, a few manufacturers make three-wheeled band saws. These have a larger throat capacity without the added weight and footprint of a saw with larger wheels. Aside from this added capacity, these saws generally perform like the small saw in the photo.perform like the small saw in the photo.

▨ *straight cuts*

Making a straight cut with a band saw is pretty much intuitive. You simply need to draw a line on your workpiece and follow it as you push the piece past the blade. A few tricks shown in the photos here may help, particularly if you are making multiple cuts. Note, in general, wider blades make cutting straight easier.

One thing you may notice when you make a straight cut is that instead of remaining parallel to the side of the table, the cut tends to wander to one side or the other. This is a problem known as blade lead, or drift. It may occur because your saw is slightly out of adjustment, or it may be that the teeth on your blade are slightly duller on one side. Regardless of the cause, you need to compensate for blade drift so it doesn't spoil your workpiece.

One simple way to help keep straight cuts straight is to use your hand as a fence. Once you get the cut started, rest your hand on the saw table and guide the piece against your thumb and index finger. You can easily compensate for drift by repositioning your hand slightly.

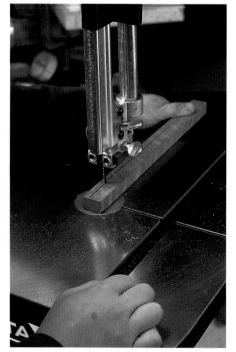
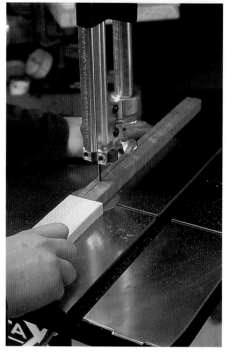

When you cut narrow pieces, the end of the cut may bring your fingers too close to the blade. In this situation, you can either reach past the blade and pull the piece through the cut (left) or push the piece through with a piece of scrap (right).

As power tools go, the band saw is relatively tame. You should, however, follow some basic safety rules.

- Keep your hands away from the line of cut. This way, should you slip, your fingers will go past the blade rather than into it.
- Use a push stick if necessary to keep your fingers away from the blade.
- Don't force the saw to cut; if you find yourself exerting a lot of pressure, stop to figure out why. Change to a sharp blade if necessary.
- Keep the piece you are cutting down on the table (see the picture on the next page).
- Keep the blade guard as low as possible as you cut.

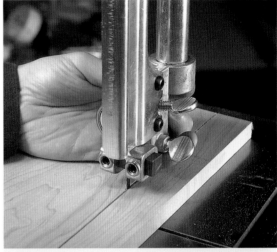

Ideally, you should adjust the blade guard so it is no more than 1/4" above the top of your workpiece. This covers as much of the blade as possible and it provides support for the blade right where it is needed.

If possible, try to plan your work so you don't have to back out of a cut. Here, when cutting the notch in this board, I made the short cut first, then the long one. This way I only had to back out a short distance.

■ JIG TIME

A Super V-Block

One of the few real hazards of the band saw comes if you try to cut wood that is un-supported by the saw's table. Because the blade exerts force downward, it will try to push anything you cut down onto the table, and it will do this with considerable force. One way many unsuspecting woodworkers learn this is when they try to cut a piece off the end of a dowel. Unless you hold the dowel with a viselike grip, the blade will spin it out of your hands. This can cause all sorts of excitement, such as broken blades and pinched fingers. Rather than run this risk, make yourself a V-block to cradle the dowel as you cut it. The block provides support right near the edge of the dowel where the blade will start cutting.

To make your V-block, use your table saw with the blade tilted to 45° and make two intersecting cuts in a 1¹/₂" x 2³/₄" x 10" block of wood.

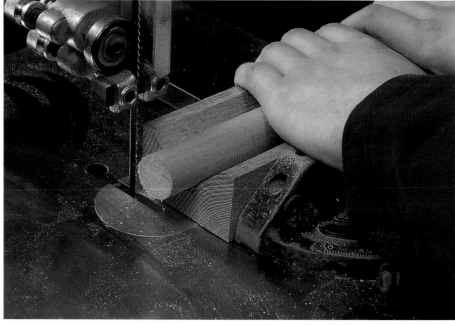

To use the V-block, hold it against the miter gauge as you push it past the blade. Cradle your workpiece in the V.

SUPER V-BLOCK

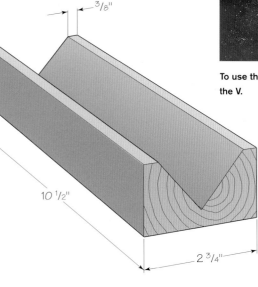

3/8"

1 ¹/₂"

10 ¹/₂"

2 ³/₄"

using a fence

Like a table saw, you can use a fence on the band saw as a guide for making straight cuts. Unlike the table saw, however, a band saw's fence is a convenience, not a necessity. Some manufacturers supply a fence with their saws or offer one as an accessory. You can also purchase a decent band saw fence from a number of other suppliers. Or, as shown on the following pages, you can make one for yourself. Regardless of where you get your fence, a key element in its operation is being able to angle it in relation to the blade to compensate for drift.

Before positioning your fence, draw a line on a piece of scrap showing the width of the pieces you want to cut. Guide the piece through the saw freehand allowing the blade to show you which way it tends to drift.

Halfway through the cut, stop the saw, leaving the board in place. If there was any drift, the board should be sitting at that angle. Clamp a straight scrap of wood aligned with the piece you are cutting.

If you use a fence a lot, it is worth the time spent to build a more permanent arrangement. Position the fence along the edge of the board, adjusting its angle to match. You should now be able to feed your stock along the fence without having to worry about drift.

A Shop-Made Fence

While you don't absolutely need a fence to cut with a band saw, having one is a great convenience. A fence makes cutting straight much easier, it allows for greater repeatability and it adds a lot of accuracy for critical cuts such as those made for joinery. Some manufacturers include a fence with their saws or offer one separately. Some fences are sold as aftermarket accessories. I decided, however, to design and make my own that includes a feature not found on any of the commercial fences I looked into: adjustability. I wanted a fence that I could adjust to compensate for blade drift. So far, I am quite pleased with the result.

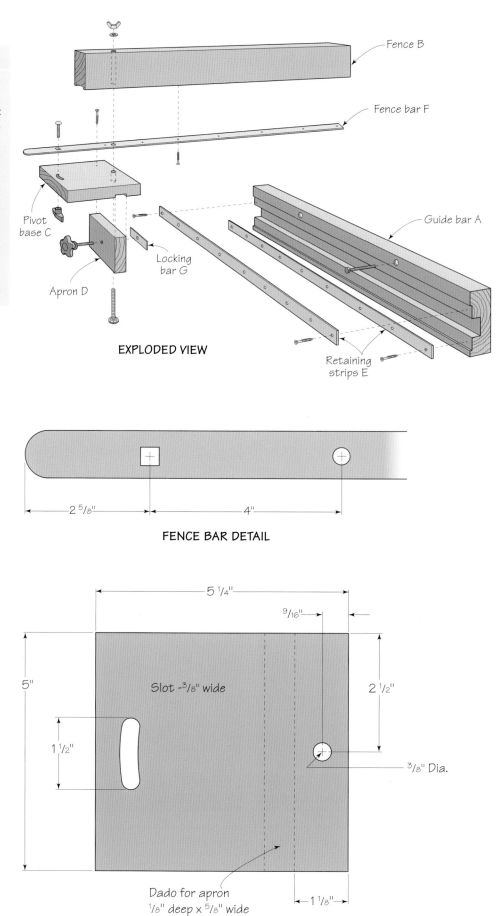

EXPLODED VIEW

Fence B

Fence bar F

Guide bar A

Pivot base C

Locking bar G

Apron D

Retaining strips E

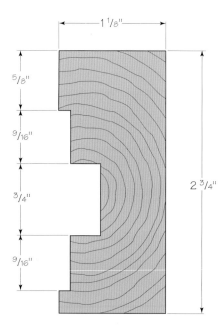

GUIDE BAR DETAIL

1 1/8"
5/8"
9/16"
3/4"
9/16"
2 3/4"

FENCE BAR DETAIL

2 5/8"
4"

PIVOT BASE DETAIL

5 1/4"
9/16"
5"
2 1/2"
1 1/2"
Slot -3/8" wide
3/8" Dia.
Dado for apron
1/8" deep x 5/8" wide
1 1/8"

REFERENCE	QUANTITY	PART	STOCK	THICKNESS	(mm)	WIDTH	(mm)	LENGTH	(mm)
A	1	guide bar	hardwood	$1^{1}/_{8}$	(29)	$2^{3}/_{4}$	(70)	30	(762)
B	1	fence	hardwood	$1^{3}/_{4}$	(45)	3	(76)	$22^{3}/_{4}$	(578)
C	1	pivot base	hardwood	$^{5}/_{8}$	(16)	$5^{1}/_{4}$	(133)	5	(127)
D	1	apron	hardwood	$^{5}/_{8}$	(16)	$2^{3}/_{4}$	(70)	5	(127)
E	2	retaining strips	steel	$^{1}/_{8}$	(3)	$^{3}/_{4}$	(19)	30	(762)
F	1	fence bar	steel	$^{1}/_{8}$	(3)	1	(25)	$27^{3}/_{4}$	(705)
G	1	locking bar	steel	$^{1}/_{8}$	(3)	$^{3}/_{4}$	(19)	$2^{3}/_{4}$	(70)

HARDWARE & SUPPLIES

1   $^{3}/_{8}$ - 16 x 4" (10mm x 80mm) carriage bolt with washer and wingnut

1   $^{3}/_{8}$ - 16 x 4" (10mm x 80mm) carriage bolt

25   No. 6 x 1" (25mm) wood screws

2   No. 6 x $1^{1}/_{4}$" (30mm) wood screws

2   $^{1}/_{4}$ - 28 x 2" (6mm x 50mm) hex-head bolts with washers

1   t-style knob with insert ($^{5}/_{16}$ - 18) Woodcraft #142226

1   knob with stud ($^{5}/_{16}$ - 18" x $1^{1}/_{2}$") Woodcraft #142906

The dimensions given here are based on a fence made for a 14" Delta X5 saw. You may need to adapt them to fit your saw.

1 Cut all the wooden pieces to the sizes given in the Materials List. Cut a dado in the face of the guide bar. The dado should be cut in three stages — two shallow cuts flanking a deeper center cut as shown in the Guide Bar Detail.

2 Use a hacksaw to cut the steel pieces to the sizes listed. File the sawn edges to smooth away any burrs.

Temporary Vise

A machinist's vise is just the ticket for doing metal work. But I didn't want to mount mine permanently to my bench. Instead I simply clamp it to a corner when I have some metal to cut.

3

Drill and countersink a series of mounting holes in the two steel retaining strips. These holes should be slightly offset to one side of the strips to compensate for the part of the strip that will overhang the center dado on the guide bar. Clamp a fence to your drill press table to help position the holes.

4

Screw the retaining strips in place on the guide bar.

5

Carefully drill mounting holes in the guide bar to match up with the holes in your saw table. Counterbore the holes if necessary so the bolt heads won't protrude past the face of the bar.

6

Grind and file the end of the fence bar to make it round. Locate the center of the square hole and center punch it as shown in the Fence Bar Detail. While you are at it, center punch the location of the pivot hole, too. Drill a 3/8" hole at the first punch mark and file it square to fit a 3/8" carriage bolt.

7

Dado the fence to accept the fence bar. Drill and countersink mounting holes along the fence bar. Screw the bar to the fence.

9

Cut a dado across the pivot base. Start small and increase the width of the dado until the apron is a snug fit.

8

Drill a ³⁄₈" hole through both the fence bar and the fence where you marked the location of the pivot hole earlier.

10

Locate the pivot hole on the pivot base. Drill a ¹⁄₄" hole here to serve as the center point for a router equipped with a trammel base. Rout the adjustment arc as shown in the Pivot Base Detail. Enlarge the pivot hole to ³⁄₈" and counterbore the underside of the base to accommodate the head of a ³⁄₈" carriage bolt.

Drill a $^5/_{16}$" hole through the apron for the locking knob. Measure carefully so the hole ends up centered over the slot in the guide bar when the apron is in place.

Glue the apron in the dado cut in the pivot base. Reinforce the joint with screws.

Drill and tap the locking bar for a $^5/_{16}$-18 thread. When you tap metal, you should always lubricate the tap with oil. Although thread cutting oil made specifically for this purpose is available, I find a general-purpose lubricant such as WD-40 works for an occasional tapping job.

using a miter gauge

Most band saws come with a slot milled into the table for a miter gauge. (Some saws even come with the miter gauge itself.) You can use the miter gauge to help control pieces as you crosscut them at any angle from about 45° to 90°. This works pretty well unless your band saw suffers from blade drift, as most do at some point or another. If you have a problem with drift, a miter gauge is not very helpful, because its track is parallel to the edge of the table, not to the cutting angle. So when you use the miter gauge, you'll actually be fighting with the way the blade wants to cut. This becomes more and more of an issue as your workpiece gets wider.

If you find drift to be a real problem, consider building the miter gauge system shown on the following pages. It can be adjusted to compensate for drift and also includes an extension fence with an adjustable stop for making repeated cuts.

Quick Cutoffs

Sometimes I have to cut a lot of pieces to roughly the same size, such as when I clean up scraps and fill my kindling boxes. Rather than measuring each piece (a bit extreme for kindling), I simply put a piece of masking tape on my saw table at the necessary distance from the blade and line up the ends of the pieces with that.

For basic cuts with the miter gauge, simply hold your work tight against the head and push the gauge past the blade.

You can easily cut many pieces to the same length by attaching a fence to the miter gauge. Then you can clamp a stop along the fence at the necessary distance from the blade.

■ **JIG TIME**

A Shop-Made Miter Gauge System

The shop-made miter gauge system consists of an auxiliary table surface with a miter gauge slot that can be pivoted to compensate for blade drift. The unit attaches to the table via a cleat that bolts to the front of the saw's table. (Note, if you built the fence system shown earlier, you can attach the miter gauge system to its guide bar.) If your saw already has a fence in place, shift the cleat so it runs along the side of the saw table. Then you can clamp the system in place there.

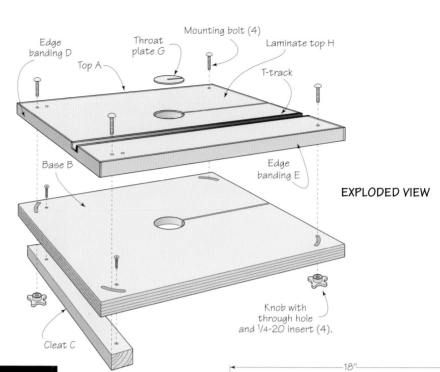

EXPLODED VIEW

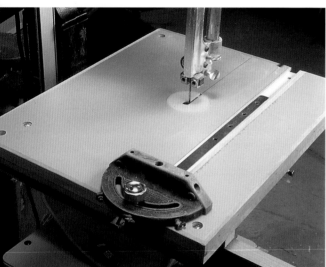

With its laminated surface and aluminum miter slot, this miter gauge system should prove accurate and durable for many years.

TOP VIEW

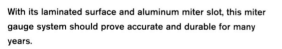

MATERIALS LIST inches (millimeters)

REFERENCE	QUANTITY	PART	STOCK	THICKNESS	(mm)	WIDTH	(mm)	LENGTH	(mm)
A	1	top	MDF	3/4	(19)	17³/8	(441)	21³/8	(543)
B	1	base	MDF	1/2	(13)	18	(457)	22	(559)
C	1	cleat	hardwood	5/8	(16)	1¹/8	(29)	18	(457)
D	2	edge banding	hardwood	5/16	(8)	3/4	(19)	18	(457)
E	2	edge banding	hardwood	5/16	(8)	3/4	(19)	21³/8	(543)
F	1	mounting cleat	hardwood	1¹/8	(29)	1¹/2	(38)	16	(406)
G	1	throat plate	acrylic plastic	1/8	(3)	3¹/2	(89)	3¹/2	(89)
H	2	laminate	HPL	1/16	(2)	18³/8	(467)	22³/8	(569)

Note, MDF is medium-density fiberboard.
Note, HPL is high-pressure laminate.

HARDWARE & SUPPLIES

	3d finish nails
4	1/4- 20 x 1¹/2" (6mm x 40mm) roundhead machine screws with washers
2	1/4- 20 x 1" (6mm x 25mm) flathead machine screws
2	1/4- 20 (6mm) threaded inserts
4	No. 8 x ³/8" (10mm) flathead wood screws
	32" T-track Woodcraft #141961
4	knobs, five star with through hole, 1/4- 20 (6mm) insert, Woodcraft #27R13
	contact cement

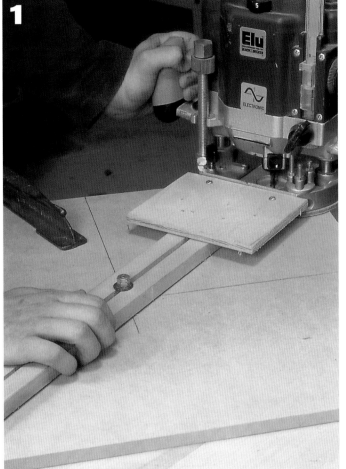

Laminate both sides of the top. Start with a piece that is slightly oversize, then cut it down to the correct dimensions as you trim the laminate flush with the edges.

Start by drilling a ¼" hole near the center of the base. Use this hole as a pivot point to rout the four curved slots near the corners of the piece. Note, you'll need to change the router setting between cutting the front and back slots.

Add edge banding to the top. Plan ahead so you can keep the nails away from the area you'll dado later for the miter gauge track.

Use a hole saw to cut the blade opening through both the top and the base.

Cut a ⅛"-deep by ⅜" rabbet around the opening you cut in the top. Cut and sand a piece of ⅛"-thick acrylic plastic to fit in the rabbet to serve as a throat plate.

Stack the base on the top to use as a guide as you drill the pivot holes through the top. Counterbore the holes in the top so the bolt heads will be recessed beneath the surface.

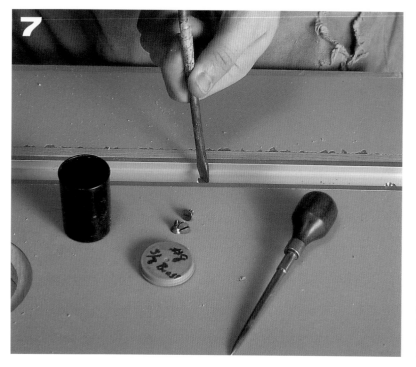

Dado the top for the miter gauge track. Measure carefully, or you may have to add a patch piece like I did (d'uh). Screw the track in place with short (⅜") screws.

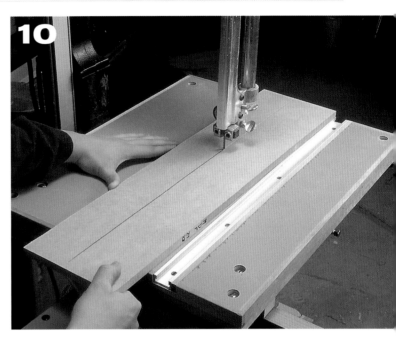

Screw the mounting cleat to the base. Drill holes through the base/cleat so you can bolt the unit to the saw. Drill matching holes through the top so you can actually tighten the mounting bolts.

To adjust the miter gauge track, cut a scrap to check which way your blade tends to lead.

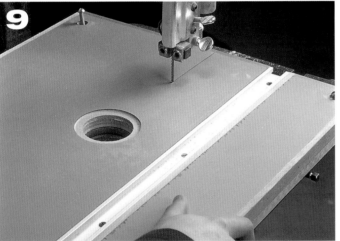

Carefully cut an access slot in from the back edge so you can mount the unit on your saw. Also cut a slot in the throat plate.

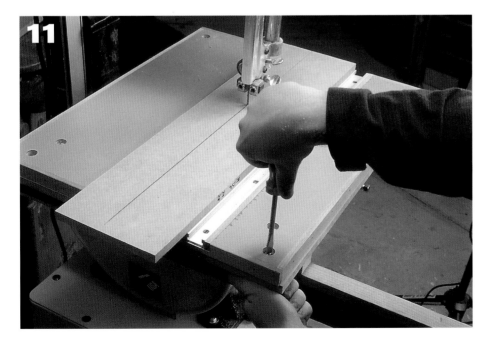

Pivot the top so the track is parallel to the edge of the test piece. Tighten the four corner knobs to lock the top in position.

▪ *making taper cuts*

Whether you're making legs for a simple Shaker table or cutting the posts for a pencil-post bed, cutting tapered pieces is an everyday event in a woodshop. It is also a job that is perfect for the band saw. If you have just one or two pieces to cut, the quickest method is to simply draw the taper on your stock, then follow the line to make the cut. If you have multiple pieces to cut, it is worth the time to make a tapering jig as shown here.

First, lay out the taper on your stock, marking exactly where you want the cut to start and stop.

The tapering jig consists of a carrier board (I use a piece of 1x8 pine) with a couple of fences screwed in place. Align your workpiece so the cut line is right along the edge of the carrier board. Screw the fences down to hold the piece in this position.

Set up a fence so the distance between it and the blade matches the width of the carrier board. Compensate for any drift if necessary (see "Using a Fence" earlier in this chapter). Make the cut by guiding the carrier board along the fence with your workpiece on top.

dealing with small pieces

Sometimes you'll have to cut pieces that are so small that holding on to them might place your fingers uncomfortably close to the blade. Here is a strategy that will make these situations a lot safer.

Tightening the Throat

Most of the time, the regular throat plate in your saw will be perfectly adequate. But sometimes you may find its opening is a little too big. This may be a problem if you are cutting small pieces, or if you are cutting something that tears out badly on the underside. In either case, the solution is to make an auxiliary table surface that performs as a zero-clearance throat plate. This is as easy as cutting a scrap of MDF to the same dimensions as your saw table. Cut into the center of the piece, then clamp it to the saw table. If the opening begins to tear, simply push the piece a little further, cutting into fresh material.

Start by attaching the workpiece to an extension board with double-sided tape or hot glue. If you use tape, a gentle squeeze with a clamp will make the joint more secure.

Once the piece is securely attached to the extension, you can cut as you usually do. Note, by placing the extension carefully, you may be able to use it as a guide in conjunction with the fence.

making curved cuts

WHILE THE BAND SAW DOES A GOOD job of making straight cuts, where it really shines is cutting curves. Whether you need to cut rockers for your grandson's new rocking horse or cabriole legs for an elegant 18th-century reproduction, the techniques shown on the following pages will help you get the most accurate results possible from your saw.

For curves where you know the radius, a compass is the tool for the job. If the curve has a larger radius, a set of trammel points that ride on a wood bar will do the trick.

laying out curves

I find one of the trickiest parts of doing curved work is actually laying out the curves. Without an accurate layout, it takes a lot of fussing to achieve any kind of a fair (smooth) curve. (Actually, even with an accurate layout, this is not exactly an easy task.) Pictured here are some of the tricks I've found that make laying out curves go a little smoother (so to speak).

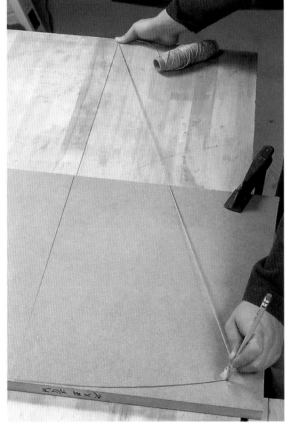

For really large diameter curves, tie a string to a pencil. Drive a nail at the center point and tie the string to it (or have a helper hold the string there). Try to keep the tension even on the string as you draw the circle.

For curves that don't have a consistent radius, a plastic drawing spline (see Hoyle Products in the suppliers list at the back of the book) is just the ticket. These flexible drawing tools are available in a variety of lengths and can be adjusted to draw a fair curve through a number of points.

Ready-Made Curves

As you get ready to lay out a curved project, don't overlook the obvious. You probably have a lot of curved objects in your shop that you can trace around quickly. It's worth keeping a mental inventory of what you have available for various radii. Finish cans, rolls of tape, washers and even coins provide useful curves.

As I was checking to make sure Hoyle still sells their adjustable splines, I discovered their Acu-Arc adjustable ruler. This tool features a flexible "straight" edge that can be bent and set at any radii from xxx to yyy.

■ JIG TIME

A Shop-Made "Bendy"

For gentle curves, you can often flex a slim strip of wood to conform to the necessary shape. Then it's a simple matter of tracing along the strip to mark your cut line. It's simple, that is, if you have a helper handy. If not, you have to resort to such gymnastics as holding the pencil in your teeth. Or you can make a "bendy" as shown in the photos. Make your bendy from a thin strip ($^1/_8$" +/-) of straight-grained wood. The straighter the grain and the more uniform the thickness, the more evenly the piece will bend. Drill a hole at either end and add a length of mason's twine to hold the curve. A little toggle at one end of the twine serves as an adjustable lock.

By adjusting the length of the string, you can flex your bendy into an infinite variety of curves. I have several lengths of bendies hanging in my shop, including a 26" and a 52".

drawing large arcs

Drawing an arc with a really large radius can be tough. I've messed around with making big compasses (unwieldy) and with tying a string to a pencil (difficult to keep from stretching the string and/or to keep everything aligned). I finally found a technique for laying out a large arc where you don't need to know the exact radius or even where the center is. What you do need to know is the distance from one end of the arc to the other (this is a straight line called a chord) and the height of the arc above the chord at any point along the arc (often at the midpoint).

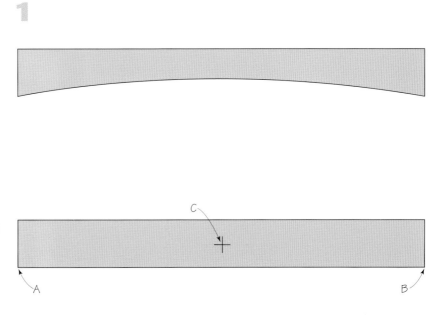

To lay out the arc shown in the top figure, mark the two ends of your arc (points A and B) on the edge your workpiece. Measure and mark the height of the arc (point C). Drive a small finish nail at both point A and point B. Try to keep these nails to the waste side of the arc.

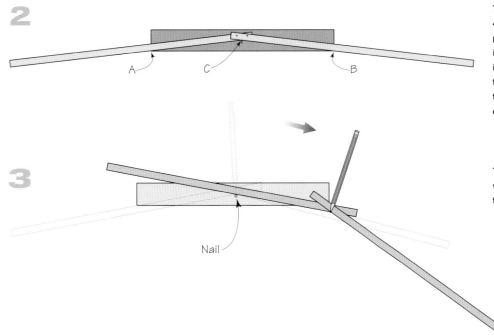

Take two straight sticks that are 3" or 4" longer than the distance from point A to point B. Place one stick so it runs from A to C, and the other so it runs from B to C. Tack the sticks together with a couple of brads so the angle between them cannot change.

To draw the arc, hold your pencil where the sticks intersect. Slowly run the sticks along the finish nails.

■ *drawing ellipses*

While circles and arcs are fine curves, they do have their limitations and may not be appropriate in all situations. You may find that the curve that looks best is one that is flatter in the center and tighter at the ends, or vice versa. You could lay out such a curve freehand, cleaning it up with a flexible spline. But if you want your design to have a more disciplined look, consider using an ellipse (or part thereof).

An ellipse (some call it an oval) is essentially a squashed circle. By varying the ratio of its width to its length, you can come up with an amazing variety of curves to suit many applications. The trick is in drawing the ellipse, and then cutting and refining the curve. A number of methods exist for drawing both true and approximate ellipses (those that look all right but are not quite true from a geometric point of view). I've included the two I find easiest and most reliable here.

Drawing an Ellipse With a Pencil and a String

This technique is relatively quick but not as precise as the second method. It is best to keep a sense of perspective when generating an ellipse this way. Your results may not be exactly what you intend, because of the difficulty in tying the string just right coupled with its inherent flexibility.

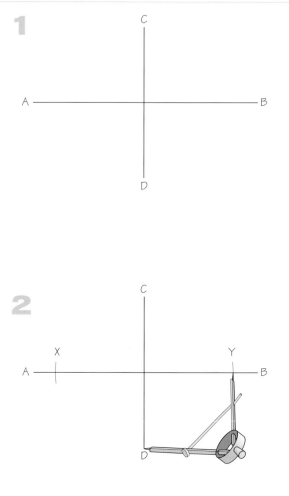

1 Start by drawing a line, AB, whose length equals the long dimension of the ellipse you desire. Locate the center point of this line and draw a second line, CD, perpendicular to the first. The length of this line should equal your ellipse's width.

2 Set a compass (or trammel) to equal half the length of AB. Place one end of the compass at point D and swing the compass to locate points X and Y along line AB. Drive small finish nails at points X and Y.

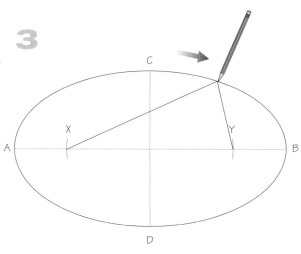

3 Tie a piece of string (mason's twine is good as it doesn't stretch very much) into a loop. The loop should reach from the nail at point X to point B. To draw the ellipse, keep the loop over both nails and stretch it taut with a pencil. Try to hold the pencil straight up and down as you draw. I find a mechanical pencil works best for this trick.

Drawing an Ellipse With a Trammel Bar

While more time-consuming, this method of drawing an ellipse yields a more predictable and precise result.

1

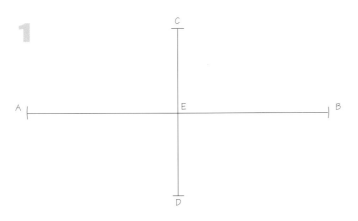

Start by drawing two perpendicular lines, AB and CD, that intersect at their midpoints (point E). The length of AB should equal the length of your ellipse, and CD, the width.

2

Place the square corner of a piece of scrap ¼" plywood in one of the corners formed by the intersecting lines. The edges of the plywood should be at least as long as the lines. You can also use a framing square as long as the ellipse is small enough. Clamp or tape the plywood in place.

3

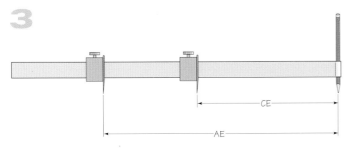

Tape a pencil to the end of your trammel bar. Set one of the two points so that the distance from the point to the pencil equals half the width of the ellipse (distance CE). Set the other point so that the distance from it to the pencil equals half the length (distance AE).

4

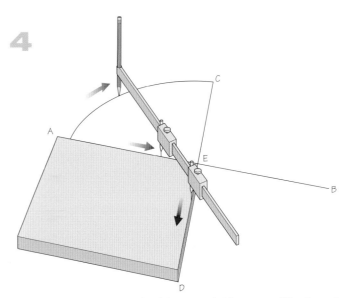

Start drawing with the inner point of the trammel at the corner of the plywood and the outer point along the edge running along line CD. Carefully move the inner point along the edge of the plywood toward point B while keeping the other point against the other edge of the plywood. Stop when this point reaches the center. Repeat the process for the other three quadrants of the ellipse.

cutting curves

Once you have the curve laid out, it's time to cut. In most instances, cutting curves requires a fairly narrow blade. I generally keep ¼" blades on hand for most curved work. However, for a shallow curve, such as those on the rockers of a rocking chair, you may find it easier to cut a smooth curve with a wider blade — say ⅜" or even ½". What follows are some suggestions for cutting curves as smoothly and accurately as possible.

One of the most common mistakes beginners make is to start cutting a curve in the wrong direction. Rather than cutting into the curve as shown here…

…start cutting as parallel as possible to the curve, then gradually turn the piece so the cut follows the line.

With tight and/or intricate curves, you may find it advantageous to make a series of straight cuts in through the waste areas. These are called relief cuts and should extend almost to the layout line. As you cut, the relief cuts will allow the waste to come free, creating more room for the blade.

As you work, try to leave a little material outside your layout line. It doesn't need to be much; a thin ¹⁄₁₆" is plenty.

When it comes to outside curves, a belt or disc sander is the perfect tool to do the final cleanup. Use a light touch and keep your piece moving to avoid facets.

Instant Drum Sander

For a quick drum sander, make a 2" cut lengthwise in a ½" dowel. Then insert a strip of sandpaper. Chuck the whole mess in your drill press. As you sand, the paper will wrap around the dowel, forming a sanding drum.

hot tip

For inside curves, an oscillating spindle sander does a marvelous job of cleaning up the saw marks. In a pinch, you can also use a sanding drum chucked in your drill press.

cutting circles

Cutting a circle on the band saw can be as simple as cutting close to your line and then sanding to the final shape. As with most operations, this works fine if you are cutting only a few circles. But if you have a lot of circles to cut for a specific job, or you cut circles on a regular basis, you will probably find it helpful to build a circle-cutting jig.

A circle-cutting jig acts essentially like a big compass, with an adjustable center pivot point. To use the jig, you set the distance from the blade to the pivot to the desired radius. Then you drill a pivot hole in the underside of your workpiece. (Note, if you don't want a hole in your workpiece, you can attach a scrap of plywood with double-sided tape and drill the picot hole in the scrap. This approach requires you to also add a spacer of equal thickness near the blade.) Place the workpiece on the pivot point, then slide the jig onto the saw. When the jig hits the corner stop, pivot the workpiece to make the cut.

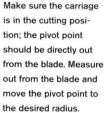

Make sure the carriage is in the cutting position; the pivot point should be directly out from the blade. Measure out from the blade and move the pivot point to the desired radius.

Cut your blank about ¼" larger than the diameter of your circle. Drill a shallow ⅛" hole at the center point. Pull the carriage to the loading position (toward the front of the saw) and place the blank on the pivot point. With a large piece, you may need to hold it at a slight angle to the blade.

Push the carriage forward until it stops in the cutting position. Slowly turn the blank on the pivot, cutting the circle. When you are finished, back the carriage up so you can lift the piece free of the pivot point.

A Circle-Cutting Jig

This jig features an adjustable pivot point that you can set the appropriate distance from the blade and a sliding carriage which lets you load your workpiece onto the jig while it is away from the blade. The hold down clamps to the table and serves two purposes. One, it positions the whole jig in relationship to the blade. Two, it serves as a hold down (hence its name), keeping the jig from tipping off the table as you cut.

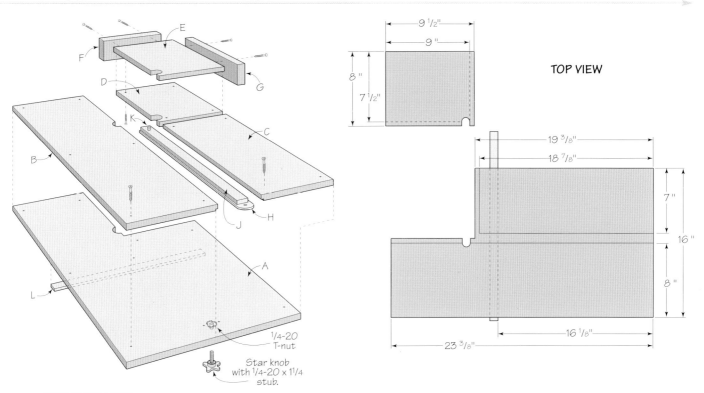

TOP VIEW

EXPLODED VIEW

MATERIALS LIST inches (millimeters)

REFERENCE	QUANTITY	PART	STOCK	THICKNESS	(mm)	WIDTH	(mm)	LENGTH	(mm)	LENGTH
A	1	base	plywood	$3/4$	(19)	16	(406)	$28^3/8$	(721)	
B	1	front top piece	plywood	$3/4$	(19)	8	(203)	$28^3/8$	(721)	
C	1	back top piece	plywood	$3/4$	(19)	7	(178)	$18^7/8$	(479)	
D	1	hold-down base	plywood	$3/4$	(19)	$7^1/2$	(191)	9	(229)	Use plywood cut off from base.
E	1	hold-down top	plywood	$3/4$	(19)	8	(203)	$9^1/2$	(241)	
F	1	locating strip	plywood	$3/4$	(19)	3	(76)	$7^3/4$	(197)	
G	1	locating strip	plywood	$3/4$	(19)	3	(76)	8	(203)	
H	1	slide	aluminum	$1/8$	(3)	$1^1/2$	(38)	20	(508)	
J	1	pivot bar	hardwood	$5/8$	(16)	1	(25)	$18^3/4$	(476)	
K	1	pivot point	dowel	$1/4$ dia.	(6 dia.)			$1/2$	(13)	
L	1	runner	hardwood	$3/8$	(10)	$3/4$	(19)	20	(508)	

HARDWARE & SUPPLIES

18 No. 8 x $1/4$" (6mm) flathead wood screws

5 No. 6 x $5/8$" (16mm) flathead wood screws

5 No. 6 x 1" (25mm) flathead wood screws

1

Start by cutting the corner off the base. Save the cutoff piece, as it will become the hold-down base.

2

Screw the hold-down top to the cutoff from step 1. The pieces should be flush along two adjacent edges. (Study the drawing to make sure you choose the correct orientation of the pieces; it is possible to get it backward.) Place a couple of playing cards in between the pieces for clearance when the rest of the jig has to slide underneath. Add the two locating strips along the flush edges. Relieve the edges of the hold-down so the jig won't hang up as you slide it into position.

3

Rabbet the edges of the top pieces. The rabbets should be a little over 1/4" wide and 1/8" deep. Note, a rabbet fence is simply a piece of scrap screwed to your table saw fence. With it in place, you can bury a portion of a wide dado setup in the fence, exposing only as much of the blade as you need.

4

Drill and countersink a series of holes in the aluminum slide. Center the pivot bar on the slide and clamp it in place. Attach the aluminum to the pivot bar with 5/8" screws. Drill and install the pivot point near one end of the pivot bar.

5

Place the top pieces on the base with the pivot bar in between them. Screw the top pieces in place.

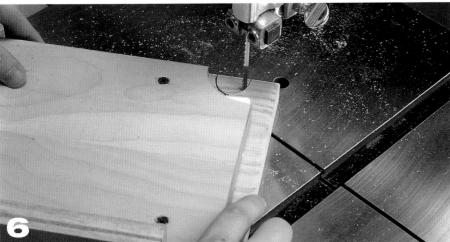

6

Cut the inside corner off the corner stop to provide clearance for the blade. Also cut a notch in the mating corner of the base unit.

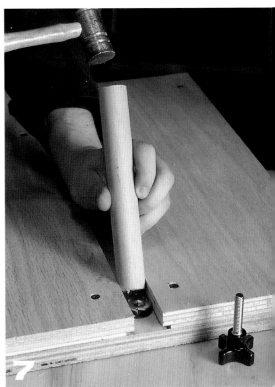

7

Drill through the base and install the T-nut near the outside end of the slot between the two top pieces.

8

Clamp the corner stop to the saw and slide the base unit into position. Carefully mark the position of the miter gauge slot on the underside of the base. Screw the runner to the base so it will fit in the slot.

cutting with a template

If you have more than two or three pieces to cut to the same shape, you may find it worth the time to make a template. Then, with the assistance of a simple follower, you can cut as many pieces as you need without the bother of laying each piece out. The template can be quite simple or more sophisticated, depending on how many pieces you need to cut.

Record Keeping Made Easy

When I build templates and jigs I intend to use later, I write the important information about using the jig right on them. This includes information such as the blank size. This saves a lot of rethinking when I get back to using the jig.

For a run of less than a dozen or so pieces, simply cut the template from a piece of ¼" or ½" material such as MDF and fasten it to your workpiece with double-sided tape.

For a bigger run, or for pieces you intend to make more of in the future, you may want to invest a little more time in making the template. This template setup features a carrier board with attached fences. The workpiece and the template get sandwiched in place with a toggle clamp.

Because of the rather benign nature of the band saw, your template doesn't have to be fastened as securely as you would need it if you were cutting with a router. Here, I used a pair of cheap hinges to locate the template on the jig. A pair of wedges locks the workpiece in place.

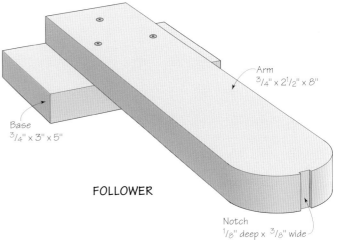

Arm
$3/4" \times 2^{1}/2" \times 8"$

Base
$3/4" \times 3" \times 5"$

FOLLOWER

Notch
$1/8"$ deep $\times$ $3/8"$ wide

Regardless of how you fasten the template to your workpiece, cutting involves clamping the follower to your saw table with the notch surrounding the blade. Use spacers as necessary to provide clearance. Cut the piece by guiding the template against the follower.

cutting multiple curves

Most woodworkers realize that cutting multiple straight pieces is generally not a big deal once you have an initial straight edge to follow. Set up a fence or clamp a stop block on the miter gauge and cut away. Cutting multiple curved pieces can be accomplished in a similar manner using a regular fence for simple curves and a single-point fence for compound curves.

To cut a series of pieces to the same curvature, lay out and make the initial cut freehand.

Measure and lock the fence the necessary distance from the blade. Cut the subsequent pieces by running the curved side of the rip fence against the fence. As long as the curve isn't too severe, the pieces you'll produce will be practically identical.

To cut a more complex curve, such as this piece of gooseneck moulding, set up a single-point fence the necessary distance from the blade. Then guide the piece through the cut.

Concave Fence

Occasionally you'll need to make a series of pieces with concave cuts, say for the aprons of a series of tables. These cuts can be made quite quickly with a concave fence that references from the corners of the workpiece. To figure out what radius curve to cut the fence to, make a full-size layout of the part as shown.

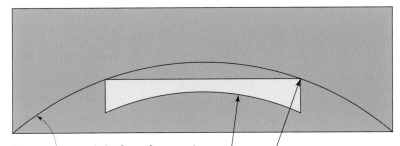

Be sure to extend the fence far enough on either side of the cut so you can start and complete the cut with the workpiece in contact with the fence.

CONCAVE FENCE DETAIL

Use the same centerpoint to lay out the radius of the cut and the radius of the fence.

Once you have the fence made, cutting a lot of pieces to the same curve is quite easy.

resawing

RESAWING IS THE ACT OF CUTTING a relatively thick board into thinner pieces. You might want to do this to make veneer from a piece with spectacular grain, or simply to avoid a lot of waste from planing down 4/4 stock to make thin drawer sides. Regardless of your intent, the process is pretty much the same: Set up a fence as a guide, then push your piece through the cut.

Because resawing involves cutting through the width of a board, it will really put your saw to the test. The wider the piece is that you try to cut, and the thinner slices you want to make, the more trouble you are likely to have. For the fewest headaches, you'll want to have a sharp, clean blade installed and have the saw tuned as well as you can get it. Chapter six, "Maintenance and Tune-Up," has details on these critical matters.

basic resawing

Perhaps the simplest approach to resawing is simply to clamp a straight scrap of wood to your saw table to use as a fence to guide your workpiece through the cut. This scrap can be a piece you grab from the cutoff bin, or it can be a piece you save for periodic use as a straightedge. In either case, the piece should be truly straight, and the face you guide your piece against should be square to the table and parallel to the blade.

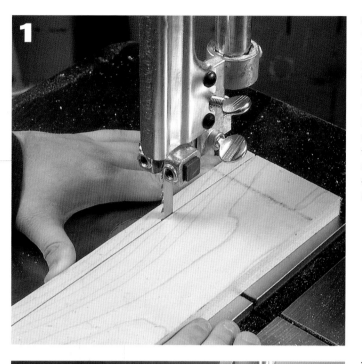

Start by cutting a scrap to the same thickness you want your finished piece. Draw a line on the edge of the scrap to follow as you cut. When you are about halfway through the cut, stop and shut off the saw, leaving the scrap in place to indicate the direction the blade drifts.

Clamp the straightedge to the saw table with its good edge against your test piece. I have a 2"-thick by 6"-wide piece of pine that I keep especially for use as a fence.

To cut the good pieces, guide them along the fence past the blade. Listen to the sounds the saw makes and keep an eye on the blade as you cut. You'll soon develop an ear for what the saw sounds like if it is cutting well. If the cut seems to wander out of line, try reducing the feed speed. You may also need to adjust the angle of the fence.

using a single-point fence

Single-Point Fence

All fences have one inherent weakness: If the fence is much taller than the workpiece, it will force you to have the blade guard set a lot higher than is necessary for both safety and accuracy. This fence system addresses this issue by including a series of fences of different heights. The lower fences are solid wood, which wears better, while the taller fences are plywood, which is easier to come by in the dimensions required.

Some woodworkers prefer to resaw using a single-point fence rather than a straight-edge. A single-point fence allows you to steer the board as you cut, thus compensating for any drift or wandering as you go. The fence shown here has an extended plywood base that makes it easy to clamp to the saw table. The exact dimensions are not critical; try to mount the fence so the point ends up aligned with the teeth on the blade or slightly in front of them.

When I made this fence system, I made four different fences for cutting pieces of various widths. All the fences use the same mounting holes.

The setup for a single-point fence is straightforward. Simply set it the desired distance from the fence. As you feed your stock through the cut, hold your left hand on the table with your fingers spread as shown. This will serve as a secondary "fence" to help keep your cut consistent.

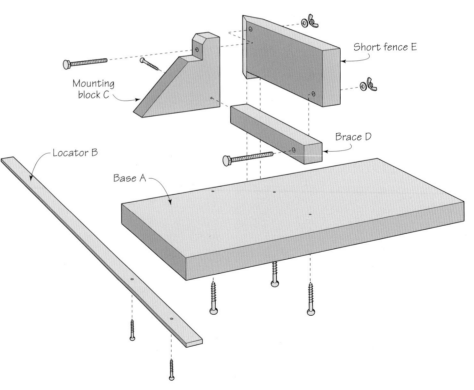

Short fence E

Mounting block C

Brace D

Locator B

Base A

A Resawing Face

This resawing face is an accessory you can add to the fence system detailed in "A Shop-Made Fence" in chapter one. It consists of a piece of hardwood plywood bolted to the regular fence to increase its height. To attach the resawing face to the regular fence, you'll need to add two threaded inserts to the fence, then drill two mounting holes in the plywood.

MATERIALS LIST inches (millimeters)

REFERENCE	QUANTITY	PART	STOCK	THICKNESS	(mm)	WIDTH	(mm)	LENGTH	(mm)
A	1	base	plywood	$^3/_4$	(19)	6	(152)	17	(432)
B	1	locator	hardwood	$^1/_2$	(13)	$1^1/_8$	(29)	16	(406)
C	1	mounting block	hardwood	1	(25)	$1^1/_2$	(38)	$5^1/_4$	(133)
D	1	brace	plywood	$^3/_4$	(19)	$4^1/_8$	(105)	$4^1/_4$	(108)
E	1	short fence	hardwood	$^3/_4$	(19)	$2^1/_4$	(57)	$6^3/_4$	(172)
F	1	medium fence	hardwood	$^3/_4$	(19)	5	(127)	$6^3/_4$	(172)
G	1	taller fence	plywood	$^3/_4$	(19)	$6^3/_4$	(172)	8	(203)
H	1	tallest fence	plywood	$^3/_4$	(19)	$6^3/_4$	(172)	11	(279)

HARDWARE & SUPPLIES

4 No. 8 x $1^5/_8$" (41mm) screws

2 No. 6 x 1" (25mm) screws

2 $5^{15}/_{16}$" x $2^1/_2$" (152mm x 64mm) carriage bolts with washers and wingnuts

Assisted Resawing

hot tip

If you find your band saw is a little lacking in the power department, you may have trouble resawing wide pieces without the saw bogging down. To help out, start resawing by cutting the pieces on your table saw first. Not only do the resulting kerfs mean there is less wood for your band saw to plow through, they will also help keep the resaw cut going straight.

The resawing face is simply a flat piece of hardwood plywood bolted to the regular rip fence.

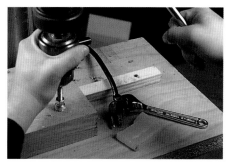

Threaded inserts make a great way of attaching temporary accessories, but they can be difficult to install. The best way I have found is to cut the head off a bolt of the appropriate size. Thread a nut onto the bolt and then thread on the insert. Chuck the whole mess in your drill press and twist the insert in its hole by hand while applying downward pressure with the quill. Note, be sure to unplug the drill press first.

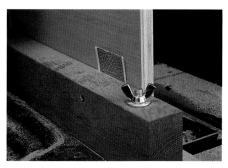

When you set up the fence, you may find the face of the fence is not parallel to the blade. If this is the case, you can add shims between the fence and the regular face to rectify the situation.

cutting veneers

Resawing a board into a series of thin veneers is not a lot different from resawing a piece in half, except that the fence is set much closer to the blade. A well-tuned band saw with adequate power and a sharp blade is capable of sawing veneer between $\frac{1}{8}$"- and $\frac{1}{16}$"-thick with ease. (If you are really fussy, you may even be able to go thinner.) The real key is in getting your saw tuned up perfectly (see chapter six, "Maintenance and Tune-Up"). Another trick I have found to be helpful is to build a specific resawing face that I attach to my rip fence (see "A Shop-Made Fence" in chapter one). By adding such a face to the fence, you combine the ease of adjustment the fence supplies with a tall surface that provides great support to your workpiece.

Slide the resaw face into place on the fence. Position the fence to leave the desired gap between the face and the blade. Resaw a scrap to check for lead. Adjusting the fence to compensate for lead is crucial when resawing thin veneers.

Mix and Match

Working with veneer gives you a great opportunity to play with the way the grain appears on your projects. Because the grain pattern on each subsequent piece of veneer sawn from a board will be more or less identical to the one that came before, you can arrange the veneers on a panel to take advantage of this. Some classic matches are shown in the photos on the following page.

It doesn't take much misalignment to cause trouble when resawing veneer. If you find the veneer coming away from the fence (and the veneer getting too thin), the fence is angled too much away from the blade. If the veneer starts to get thicker, the fence may not be angled quite enough.

If you open the veneers like pages of a book, you create what is called a bookmatch. Bookmatching yields symmetrical panels that have a balanced feel.

Placing each veneer in the same orientation creates what is called a slipmatch. Slipmatches get away from the predictability and balance of a bookmatch.

By combining both bookmatches and slipmatches, you can create some pleasing effects.

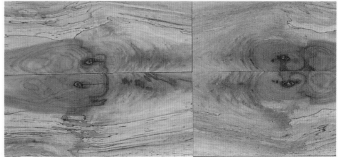

Bookmatching pieces both side to side and end to end makes panels that look contained and elegant.

working with veneer

Sawing your own veneer is but a small part of the job. Once you cut the pieces, a number of steps follow before you can glue them in place. While there is much more to the craft of veneering than I have space for here, the following pictures should give you a start. Note, if you use a fresh, sharp blade and your saw is tuned well, you may be able to glue the veneer down without having to do anything to its surface other than brushing aside the dust. Also note that whenever you veneer, you should apply veneer to both sides of a panel to keep it balanced. Otherwise the panel is likely to warp.

If you cut your veneer on the thick side ($^1/_8$" +/-) and the grain isn't too wild, you can surface it with your planer. If necessary, slip a belly board (a piece of plywood with a plastic laminate surface) through the machine so you can cut the thin pieces.

An alternative to a planer is to run the pieces through a drum sander. With thin pieces, it often works best to run them through on a carrier board (a fancy name for a scrap of plywood). If the pieces slip, try adding a short heel to the back of the carrier, or stick the pieces down with double–sided tape.

If you intend to join two or more pieces of veneer together edge to edge, you'll need to joint the adjoining edges much as you would for making an edge joint in thicker stock. To help hold on to the thin pieces, capture them face-to-face between two pieces of plywood. Make sure the bottom edges of the veneers are protruding below the plywood, then run the whole sandwich over the jointer.

2a

If you don't have a jointer, you can achieve the same thing if you run the pieces past a flush-trim bit chucked up in your table-mounted router. Make sure the edges of the plywood are smooth and straight, as that is what will determine how straight the veneer ends up.

3

Once the edges are straight, you'll need to tape the veneers together before gluing them down. Hold the pieces next to each other to check the fit. The edges should go together without having to coax them at all. Apply strips of tape across the seam to hold the pieces together. Veneer tape (a paper tape with a water-soluble adhesive) is best, but masking tape will work.

■ JIG TIME
A Veneer Jointing Jig

This jig consists of two pieces of plywood joined with knobs that thread into T-nuts. Make the jig long enough to accommodate your longest pieces of veneer.

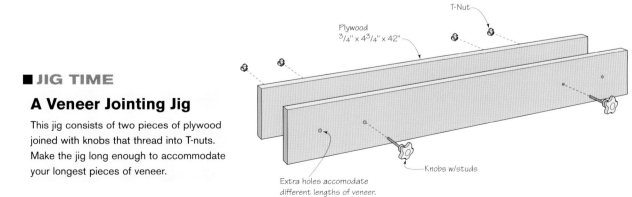

T-Nut

Plywood
³/4" x 4³/4" x 42"

Knobs w/studs

Extra holes accomodate
different lengths of veneer.

(WORKING WITH VENEER CONTINUED)

What Not to Glue

Never apply glue directly to the veneer. The moisture in the glue will almost immediately affect the thin material, causing it to warp and curl uncontrollably.

Cut your substrate to size. Both MDF (medium-density fiberboard) and hardwood plywood make good substrates. Apply glue to both sides of the substrate and spread it evenly. I use a printer's brayer (a hard rubber roller) for this process. Triangular strips keep the glue off of your bench.

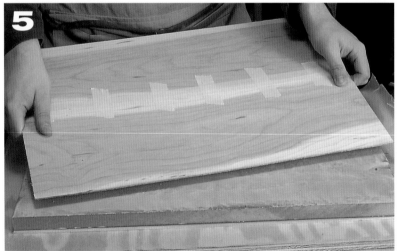

You'll also need two pieces of plywood that are slightly larger than your panel. Have these ready before you apply the glue. Cover one with waxed paper, then place your veneer on top (any tape should be toward the outside). Set the substrate in place and quickly add the other piece of veneer, followed by more waxed paper and the second piece of plywood.

Clamp the whole stack together. If the stack is less than 12" wide, you can simply squeeze it directly with clamps. If the stack is much wider, make some cauls from hardwood sticks, about 1½" x 2" x whatever length, to help distribute the clamping pressure evenly across the panel.

Air Bags in the Woodshop?

TOOL TALK

Another option for clamping veneered panels is to press them in a vacuum bag. These systems are available commercially, or you can build your own at a considerable savings. I found a great set of plans on the Internet at www.joewoodworker.com. If you do more than the occasional veneer job, a vacuum bag system is well worth it.

cutting lumber

Another way to use your band saw is as a small sawmill. This is much like resawing, except there is no "re" about it. The trick here is to build some kind of a jig or carriage to hold the logs as you saw them. Depending on your access to logs, the accessibility of your shop, and your ambition, you can saw some pretty big material using this method. Other than the size of your saw, the biggest problem to overcome is the weight of the logs themselves. Before you get carried away, consider this: While you may be able to fit a 10" or 12" log through your saw, an 8' log of oak, 10" in diameter, is going to weigh several hundred pounds. You'll need some added support to help hold the log as you cut it, and a couple of strong helpers to position the log and muscle it through the cut. The setup shown here is designed to handle more modest pieces, but it could be scaled up to handle bigger logs.

After you cut your logs, paint the ends as soon as possible to minimize checking. This is a great way to use up leftover paint.

Before sawing the logs, strip away the bark. I use a drawknife for this, but a wide chisel also works well. Removing the bark helps keep your band saw blades sharper by getting rid of any dirt and grit that may have been embedded in the bark as the log traveled from the forest to your shop. Save the bark for your favorite gardener. Who can resist hand-hewn mulch?

Attach the log to the carriage with lag screws. The lag screws don't have to stick very far into the log — only ³/₄" or so; they are there just to keep the log from shifting as you cut.

4

Adjust the carriage so about 1$\frac{1}{2}$" of the log overhangs the edge. Adjust the fence on the table to cut this overhanging portion off the log. Guide the carriage along the fence to make the cut.

5

Unbolt the log and turn it so the surface you just cut is down on the base of the carriage. Drive the lags back in to hold the log in place. Reset the fence and make a second cut, creating a second surface that is square to the first.

6

Once you have two flat surfaces, you no longer need to mount the log on the carriage. Instead, use the carriage as a fence. Clamp it to the table, leaving a space between it and the blade equal to the thickness of the boards you are after. Guide the log along the fence to make the cuts.

7

When you finish cutting the log, you'll need to sticker the boards while they dry. Cut a number of strips of wood about $\frac{1}{2}$" thick and a little longer than your pieces are wide. Stack the boards with stickers in between each piece spaced about 16" apart. Make the pile in an out-of-the-way place — covered and dry, but not necessarily heated. Wood generally air-dries at the rate of about 1" of thickness per year. After a year (for 1" stock), bring the pieces into your shop to allow them to acclimate for at least two weeks; four or six weeks is even better. Then cut a test piece. If it seems to stay flat and straight, you're probably ready to go. If it warps a lot, more drying may be necessary.

Sawmill Conversion

Turning your band saw into a sawmill isn't all that difficult. Mostly what this conversion does is provide a larger table to make it easier to support heavy logs. The table is, in turn, supported by an outrigger that is bolted to the machine's base. When I designed this setup, I originally thought about having support stands that rested on the floor. But because I move my saw around a lot, I wanted the whole setup to be a little more portable. So having the whole thing attached to the saw seemed like the way to go. In using the rig, I have found this works pretty well, though I am considering adding some fold-down legs for a little extra stability.

With its large extension table and built-in fence, this sawmill setup makes it relatively easy to cut logs into usable lumber. While I have listed specific sizes and whatnot, don't worry too much about duplicating my setup exactly. I just used the materials I had on hand. Make your rig to suit your saw.

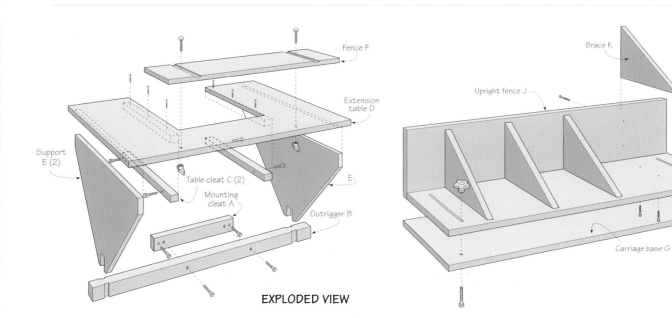

EXPLODED VIEW

MATERIALS LIST inches (millimeters)

REFERENCE	QUANTITY	PART	STOCK	THICKNESS	(mm)	WIDTH	(mm)	LENGTH	(mm)	LENGTH
A	1	mounting cleat	hardwood	$1^1/_8$	(29)	$2^3/_4$	(70)	16	(406)	
B	1	outrigger	hardwood	$1^1/_2$	(38)	$2^3/_4$	(70)	48	(1219)	
C	2	table cleats	hardwood	$1^1/_8$	(29)	$1^1/_4$	(32)	16	(406)	
D	1	extension table	plywood	$3/_4$	(19)	24	(610)	48	(1219)	covered on both sides with plastic laminate, ¼" edging
E	2	supports	plywood	$3/_4$	(19)	22	(559)	20	(508)	
F	1	fence	plywood	$3/_4$	(19)	$5^3/_4$	(146)	34	(864)	
G	1	carriage base	plywood	$3/_4$	(19)	12	(305)	48	(1219)	
H	1	carriage fence base	plywood	$3/_4$	(19)	8	(203)	48	(1219)	
J	1	upright fence	plywood	$3/_4$	(19)	8	(203)	48	(1219)	
K	1	brace	plywood	$3/_4$	(19)	$6^1/_2$	(165)	7	(178)	

HARDWARE & SUPPLIES

2   $1/_4$-20 x 2" (6mm x 50mm) bolts with washers and nuts (to attach mounting cleat to saw)

2   $1/_4$-20 x 21/2" (6mm x 60mm) bolts with threaded inserts (to attach outrigger to cleat)

4   $1/_4$-28 x 2" (6mm x 50mm) bolts (to attach table cleats to table)

30 No. 8 x $1^5/_8$" (41mm) screws

   $3/_8$-16 x 2" (10mm x 50mm) carriage bolts with knobs

Once I decided how I wanted the sawmill jig to work, the hardest part was working up the nerve to drill holes into the base of a brand-new saw. After that, drilling the holes was a straightforward operation. Drill the holes in the ledger first, then clamp the ledger in place and use it as a guide to drill the holes in the saw.

Install threaded inserts (visible in the previous photo) in the ledger, then bolt the outrigger in place using these inserts. Cut notches in the ends of the outrigger to hold the supports.

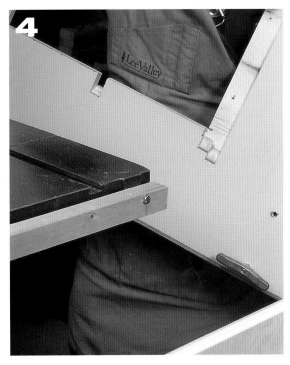

Add table cleats to the saw table to support the extension table. Bolt the cleats in place using the holes meant to attach a fence to the saw.

Depending on the relative height of the table cleats, you may need to rabbet the underside of the extension table so it ends up level with the saw's table. Don't worry about rabbeting too deep; you can always add a shim or two to bring the table up a little if need be.

joinery

YOUR BAND SAW CAN BE AN INVALU-
able tool when it comes to cutting joints. At
its most basic, you can think of it as a big
handsaw, albeit one with an electric motor.
Because most joinery involves making straight
cuts, as long as you can saw straight, you can
make these cuts on the band saw. Adding a
fence makes sawing straight even easier, plus it
adds the possibility of making repeat cuts. Add
in some stop blocks along with a jig or two,
and you can turn your saw into a precision
joint-making machine.

cutting lap joints

One of the simplest ways to put two pieces of wood together is with a lap joint. You can use lap joints to assemble simple frames, as well as the parts for a basic chair or stool. You can cut a lap joint to join pieces at their ends, or anywhere in between.

While they are not the most sophisticated-looking joints, lap joints can be cut quickly and are quite strong.

Carefully lay out the cuts on the pieces to be joined. Typically, you should plan to remove half the thickness of each piece.

Make the shoulder cuts by guiding the pieces into the blade with the miter gauge. If you have more than one or two joints to cut, you'll probably find it worth setting up some stop blocks to control the length of the lap and the depth of the shoulder cut.

Make the cheek cut by running the piece along the fence. I usually have several test pieces prepared, the same width and thickness as my good stock, so I can test my setup first.

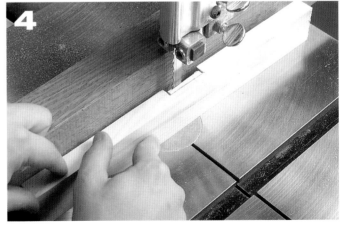

If the lap occurs in the middle of a piece, you can still use the fence. Simply make a series of shallow cuts, flipping the piece end for end, until its face rides against the fence and the recess is deep enough.

cutting mortise-and-tenon joints

Actually, this section is mostly about using the band saw to cut tenons; band saws just aren't very good at cutting mortises. The tool for mortising is the plunge router. I've included plans for my mortising jig on the next page. Generally, I'll rout the mortises first, and then cut tenons on the band saw to match.

Lay out a tenon on the end of your workpiece. I've used a sharp pencil here so the layout would show in the photo. You may find it more precise to cut the lines with a knife.

Make the shoulder cuts by guiding the piece into the blade with the miter gauge. Cut one side, then turn the piece over and cut the other. Lock the fence in place to serve as a stop so the shoulders align on either side of the piece.

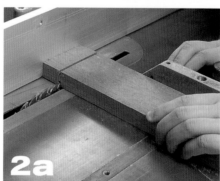

Sometimes, I'll make the shoulder cuts with my table saw. As with the band saw, use the miter gauge to guide the pieces and set the fence as a stop. While the band saw does a good job with the shoulder cuts, the table saw makes a slightly crisper cut, especially in harder woods such as maple.

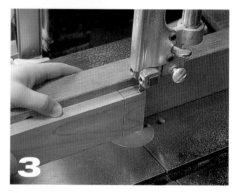

Set up the fence to make the cheek cuts. Cut the first side, then move the fence over to cut the second side.

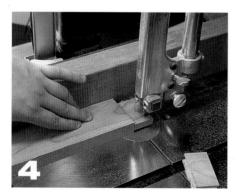

Reset the fence to cut the tenons to their final width. Make these cuts with the piece flat on the saw table.

The only problem with routing the mortises is that they end up with round ends. So you either have to round the tenons to match, or cut the mortises square with a chisel. I usually round the tenons. Use a scraper, a file or a chisel to round the corners of the tenon to fit the mortise.

A Router Mortising Jig

I built the first version of this jig almost 20 years ago and have been revising it ever since. Variations of it have appeared in a number of other books, and I offer it here because it works well and it is relatively easy to build. About the only drawback I have found is that because the router isn't fully supported, it can tip as you are cutting. As long as you are aware of this potential problem, keeping the router upright just requires a little practice.

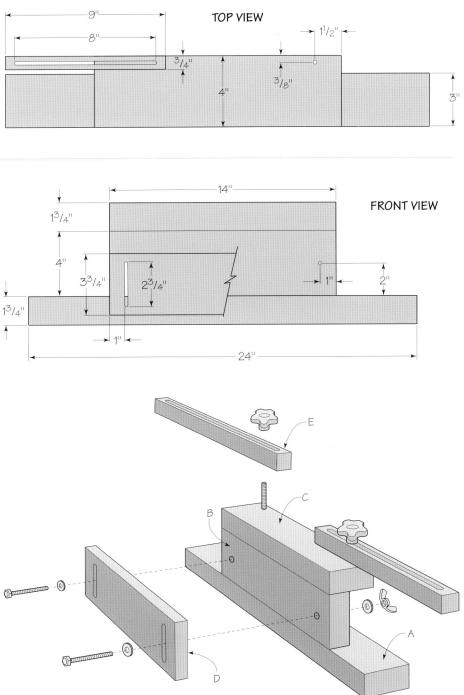

TOP VIEW

FRONT VIEW

EXPLODED VIEW

This mortising jig works hand in hand with a plunge router equipped with an edge guide. Adjustable stops on the jig control the length of the mortise, while the attached toggle clamps hold the workpiece in place. As you use the jig, it works best to cut from right to left.

MATERIALS LIST inches (millimeters)

REFERENCE	QUANTITY	PART	STOCK	THICKNESS	(mm)	WIDTH	(mm)	LENGTH	(mm)
A	1	base	hardwood	$1^3/4$	(45)	3	(76)	24	(610)
B	1	upright	hardwood	$1^3/4$	(45)	4	(102)	14	(356)
C	1	table	hardwood	$1^3/4$	(45)	4	(102)	14	(356)
D	1	fence	hardwood	$3/4$	(19)	$3^3/4$	(95)	14	(356)
E	2	stops	hardwood	$3/4$	(19)	$3/4$	(19)	9	(229)

HARDWARE & SUPPLIES

2 $3/8$-16 x $3^1/2$" (10mm x 90mm) hex-head bolts

4 $3/8$-16 x $3^1/2$" (10mm x 90mm) hex-head bolts with washers

2 $3/8$-16 x $3^1/2$" (10mm x 90mm) hex-head bolts with washers and wing nuts

2 $1/4$-20 x 3" (6mm x 80mm) hex-head bolts

2 $1/4$-20 (6mm) knobs

cutting dovetails

With its angled lines and checkerboard pattern of long and end grain, the hand-cut dovetail is, perhaps, the ultimate showcase for a woodworker's skills. The joint is also extremely strong, but it does require an investment of skill, time and practice to execute properly. The essential skill involved is the ability to saw straight. To this end, there is really no difference in substituting the band saw for your dovetail saw. The band saw will simply save you a little time and effort.

When you cut dovetails on the band saw, you have plenty of freedom to space the pins and tails as you please. If you make the depth of the sockets slightly less than the thickness of your stock, the joint will be a lot easier to glue and clean up.

Set a T-bevel to match the dovetail angle. I made a gauge from a piece of maple so I wouldn't have a lot of layout work to do. I determined the angle on the gauge by tilting the table on my band saw toward the column as far as it would go. Any angle from 6° to 10° will work.

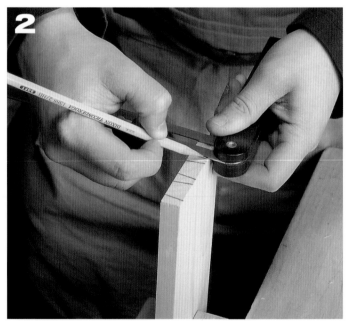

Use the T-bevel to lay out the pins on the end of one of the pieces to be joined. Traditionally, there is a half pin at either side, and the full pins in between are narrower than the tails that separate them.

Lay out the cut lines by extending the angled lines down the face of the board. Use a square to make sure the lines are perpendicular to the end of the board.

Rather than drawing the shoulder lines with a pencil, cut them with a sharp knife. Severing the surface fibers will help to create a nice, crisp shoulder line in the finished joint.

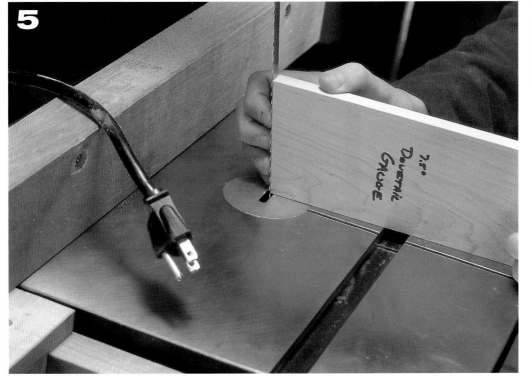

Tilt the table on your saw to match the angle on the gauge. It doesn't matter which way you tilt the table first. Once you finish the first set of cuts, you can tilt the table the opposite direction for the second set.

6

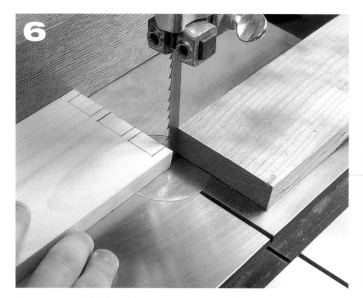

Clamp a scrap behind the blade to serve as a stop. This should stop your cut just shy of the shoulder line. Set the fence and guide the piece along it to make the cuts. To cut the half pin closest to the fence, you may raise the blade guard up above the top of the fence for clearance.

7

Reset the table so it is square to the blade. Make repeated cuts to clear away the waste between the pins. If you had to raise the blade guard to make a cut close to the fence, be smarter than me and lower the blade guard before proceeding.

8

Move back to your bench and clean up the shoulders with a sharp chisel. Work on top of a scrap to avoid scarring your bench top.

9

Mark the adjoining pieces with matching letters so you don't get them mixed up with other pieces. Also, mark the shoulder line on the tail board. Again, a sharp knife is a better choice than a pencil. Here, I cut the line, then darkened it with pencil for the photo.

10

Align the pin board on the tail board with the edges flush and the back edge of the pins resting on the shoulder line you just marked. Trace each pin with a knife to lay out the tails.

11

Mark the waste areas (trust me, it's all too easy to get confused) and cut along the knife lines to cut out the tails. Note, as you cut, keep to the waste side of the lines.

12

Saw away the waste from the half-pin sockets at the edges of the board. For the interior sockets, make repeated cuts as you did in step 7. Clean up all the shoulders with a sharp chisel.

cutting dovetails with a dovetail jig

If you intend to cut a lot of dovetails with the band saw, you may find it worthwhile to build a jig to make your results more predictable and the setup faster. Actually, the jig is two jigs — one to cut the pins and the other to cut the tails. Once you have the jigs, all you'll have to do is lay out the first joint and make a series of spacers (cut from hardboard or MDF) specific to that joint. Then you can cut as many dovetails as you desire quickly and accurately. Plans for the jigs are on this and the next page.

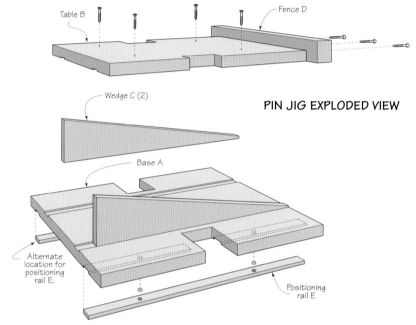

Table B   Fence D
Wedge C (2)
Base A
Alternate location for positioning rail E.
Positioning rail E

PIN JIG EXPLODED VIEW

REFERENCE	QUANTITY	PART	STOCK	THICKNESS	(mm)	WIDTH	(mm)	LENGTH	(mm)
A	1	base	plywood	3/4	(19)	13	(330)	17	(432)
B	1	table	plywood	3/4	(19)	10	(254)	15 3/4	(400)
C	2	wedges	plywood	3/4	(19)	3 1/8	(79)	15 3/4	(400)
D	1	fence	hardwood	1	(25)	1 3/4	(45)	12	(305)
E	1	positioning rail	hardwood	1/2	(13)	3/4	(19)	20	(508)

MATERIALS LIST inches (millimeters)

HARDWARE & SUPPLIES

11 No. 8 x 1 5/8" (41mm) screws

2 No. 6 x 1/2" (13mm) screws

4 1/4" (6mm) rare earth magnets with mounting cups (www.leevalley.com)

MATERIALS LIST inches (millimeters)

REFERENCE	QUANTITY	PART	STOCK	THICKNESS	(mm)	WIDTH	(mm)	LENGTH	(mm)
A	1	base	plywood	3/4	(19)	12	(305)	25 3/4	(654)
B	1	side fence	plywood	3/4	(19)	3 1/8	(79)	15 3/4	(400)
C	1	front fence	plywood	3/4	(19)	3 1/4	(82)	7 1/2	(191)

HARDWARE & SUPPLIES

3 No. 8 x 1 1/4" (32mm) screws

1 1/4-20 x 2 1/2" (6mm x 60mm) carriage bolt

1 1/4-20 (6mm) knob

2 Zero-Play Guide Bars (www.microjig.com)

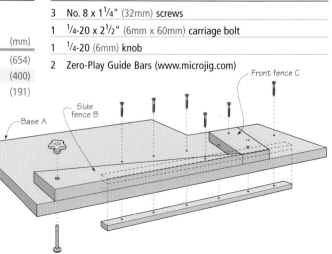

Front fence C
Side fence B
Base A

TAIL JIG EXPLODED VIEW

These two jigs are fairly easy to build. The only unusual part is the guide bar on the bottom of the tail jig. I used a pair of zero-play guide bars made by Micro Jig, Inc. While you could make this piece from a length of straight hardwood, the zero-play bar makes it quite easy to get a precise fit in the miter gauge groove.

Construction Notes

1. The wedges and the side fence should match identically. Their angles determine the dovetail angle.
2. The angle I used was 10°, but you can vary that to suit your tastes.
3. The side fence is attached with a single screw and a carriage bolt with a knob. The bolt goes through an oversized hole in the fence so you can tweak the fence to get the angle just right. As you make the jig, attach the side fence and make a test cut. Check the angle against the angle of the table on the pin jig. Adjust the side fence if necessary, then attach the front fence square to the side fence.
4. As built, the jigs will accommodate boards up to about 8" wide.

TOP VIEW

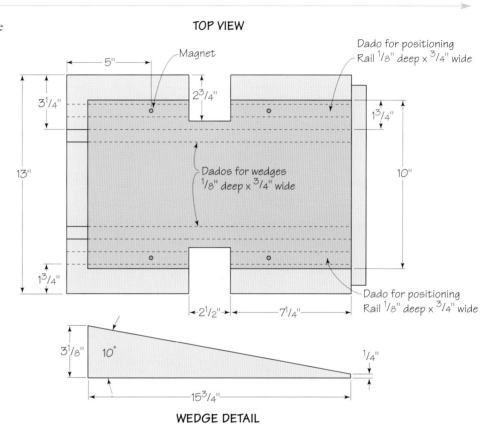

WEDGE DETAIL

TOP VIEW

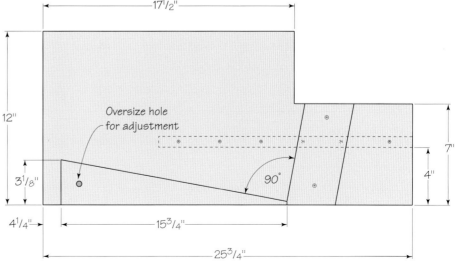

Start the process by laying out the pins on a test piece that is cut to the same dimensions as your good pieces. This system is easiest to use if the pins are evenly spaced, but as long as you can keep track of the various dimensions, there is no reason it won't work with uneven spacing.

Clamp the pin jig to the saw with the positioning rail snug against the front of the table. Clamp the stop in place, too; you can adjust it later. Place the test piece on the table with the first pin aligned with the blade. Measure the distance from the edge of the piece to the fence. Cut a spacer that matches this distance.

Make the first cut with the spacer in between the fence and the test piece. Adjust the stop so the cut ends just shy of the shoulder line.

Cut more spacers, one for each full pin in the joint. If you spaced the pins evenly, the spacers will be identical. The width of the spacers should equal the distance from the center of one pin to the center of the next. Note, sand or plane the corners of the spacers to eliminate any fuzz left over from sawing.

Make the third cut with the third spacer in place. Don't lose the spacers; you'll need them for the tail cuts. Remove the waste from between the pins.

6

Once you have one side of each pin cut, you'll have to turn the jig around to make the second cuts. The positioning rail is held to the bottom of the jig with rare earth magnets, which makes it easy to swap it to the second dado slot so you can align the jig with the inclined surface tipped in the opposite direction.

7

Place the test piece back on the jig with the initial space between it and the fence. Carefully move the jig until the blade is aligned with the layout line. Clamp the jig in place and make the first cut. Make the other cuts by adding the spacers one at a time.

8

Transfer the layout to the second test piece. Put the tail jig on the saw and place the second test piece against the front fence. Cut a spacer to align the first tail cut with the blade. Reset the stop if necessary.

9

Make the first tail cut with the spacer in place. Flip the board over and make the second cut using the same spacer.

10

The subsequent tail cuts are made using the spacers from step 4. Insert a spacer, make two cuts, flipping the piece in between, then insert the next spacer and repeat. If you need to make adjustments, insert a playing card between the fence and the spacer as a shim. Remove the waste as before and fit the joint together.

cutting round tenons

If you use dowels in your woodworking, you may need to cut tenons on their ends. This may occur when you're making stools or chairs with rungs reinforcing the legs, or if your design calls for a series of round balusters. While you can turn these tenons on a lathe or purchase a special tenoning bit for your drill, it is also possible to cut round tenons on the band saw.

Start by making the shoulder cut. Cradle the dowel in a V-block (see "A Super V-Block" in chapter one). Clamp a scrap to the table to serve as a depth stop and set the fence to control the length of the tenon. Guide the dowel into the cut with the V-block against the miter gauge. When you bump against the stop, carefully rotate the dowel against the direction of the blade to cut the shoulder, keeping a firm grip on the dowel.

Rotate the dowel slightly and make a second cut, then back out. Rotate the dowel a little more and keep cutting, then backing out.

Clamp the V-block to the fence just in front of the blade. Adjusting the fence now controls the diameter of the tenon. Move the stop block to a position behind the blade to stop the cut when it reaches the shoulder. Slide the dowel along the V-block to make the cut.

At first the tenon will be faceted, but with enough repetition, the tenon will eventually become round.

Calling for Backup

When you rout across the end of a piece, the trailing edge often splinters as the bit leaves the cut. To keep this from happening, push the piece through the cut with a push block. The push block will support the wood fibers on the trailing edge, preventing them from splintering.

making wooden hinges

Wooden hinges are fun to make, and they are useful in a variety of situations. If you make small ones, you can use them on wooden boxes. Larger ones can be used to articulate the legs on a gateleg or drop-leaf table. If you really get extreme, you can actually make the juncture of a tabletop and a leaf a big wooden hinge.

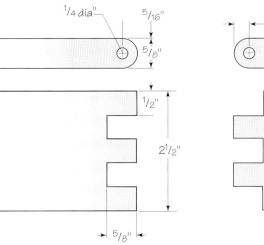

HINGE LAYOUT

The key to making good-looking, smooth-operating wooden hinges lies in the careful preparation of the stock at the beginning of the project. Decide how wide to make each finger, then make the overall hinge some odd multiple of that number. Here, the fingers are ½" wide and the overall hinge width is 2½".

Start by laying out the joint as shown in the Hinge Layout. Then round over the edges of the pieces on the router table. Don't worry about cutting away your layout lines; enough of them will be left for you to see. The radius of the roundover should be half the thickness of your stock.

Use the fence to position the piece for the first cut as shown in the Hinge Layout. Clamp a stop block behind the blade to keep from cutting too deep. Make the cut, then flip the piece over so the opposite edge is against the fence and cut again.

Carefully prepare a spacer piece that is twice the width of the fingers. (The spacer here is 1" wide; 2 x ½" = 1".) For a hinge with three fingers on one piece (and two on the other), you'll need a single spacer. For wider hinges, add an additional spacer for each additional finger (four fingers equals two spacers; five fingers equals three spacers; etc.)

Place the spacer against the fence and run the piece along it to make the next cut. Then flip the piece and make the final cut. Note, for wider hinges, repeat this process, adding spacers until all the cuts are made.

Reposition the fence to set up the saw to cut the second piece. Position the stock to make the first cut as shown in the Hinge Layout. Make the cuts as before, cutting until the piece bumps into the stop block. Flip the piece to cut the opposite side. Then make the second set of cuts with the spacer in place.

6

Make diagonal cuts through the waste areas between the fingers. Mark the waste parts first so you don't get confused and cut into some part you want to keep.

7

Switch over to a ⅛" blade. Reposition the fence to make the shoulder cuts. Sneak the piece onto the blade and guide it along the fence to cut away the remainder of the waste. Repeat with the second piece.

8

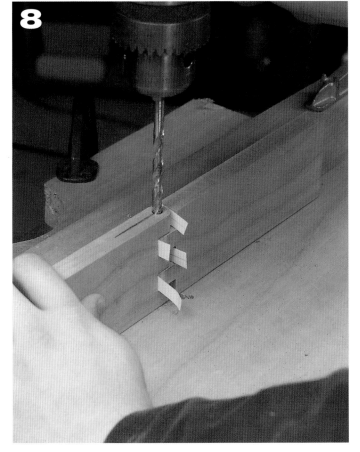

Assemble the two hinge pieces with a couple thicknesses of paper tucked in between to maintain a little clearance. Hold the pieces flat against a fence to keep them aligned as you drill the pivot pin hole. Make the diameter of the hole approximately one-third the thickness of the stock. For a hinge pin, I usually use a brass or steel rod.

chapter five

3-D cutting

AS YOU BEGIN TO GET SOME EXPERI-ence with your band saw, you'll begin to see all sorts of possibilities for intricate cuts and forms. I find some of the most intriguing shapes the band saw is capable of come from sawing through a piece multiple times. This involves making two or more series of cuts, being careful to save the cutoffs in between. After the first cut (or cuts) you reassemble everything in order and tape the whole mess back together. Then rotate the piece 90° and make a second set of cuts. Now the blade will be perpendicular to the way it was oriented the first time. After you finish cutting, peel away the taped-on bits to reveal a unique, three-dimensional object. With a little thought and practice, you can turn out some really unusual pieces this way.

making puzzles

One quick way to get some experience cutting in three dimensions is to make some puzzles. These quick, fun projects can be as simple or as complex as you care to make them. All that is required is cutting some gentle curves through a rectangular chunk of wood. As you might guess, the complexity increases with the number of cuts you make.

The most basic of these band saw puzzles requires two cuts, which yield four separate pieces. The photo shows a puzzle with nine pieces. It required a total of four cuts.

Start with a piece of wood about 1¾" square and 5" long. Make one or more curving cuts along its length. You don't need to lay the cuts out; simply cut what feels right.

Tape the pieces back together, then turn the blank so the initial saw cuts are now perpendicular to the blade. Make one or more additional cuts, cutting right through the masking tape. Try not to make these subsequent cuts match the first (although this might make the puzzle trickier). With a little sanding and a coat or two of a nontoxic finish, your puzzle should now be ready for hours of play.

cutting bowls

Another kind of three-dimensional sawing you can do is to cut bowls and containers from heavier chunks of wood. The bowl blanks can simply be pieces of firewood, offcuts from some thick boards or even thick laminations you have glued up from thinner material. If you make your bowls round, the result will be somewhat like a bowl turned on a lathe. But don't limit yourself only to circular objects. With a band saw, almost any shape is possible.

At first glance, this appears to be a wooden bowl turned on a lathe. It's not. It was made with a series of band saw cuts.

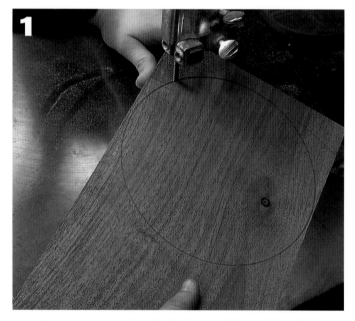

Lay out the overall shape of your bowl on the top of the workpiece. Tilt the saw table 20° or so to give the bowl a little flair. Cut out the bowl, following your layout line.

Reset the saw table so it is perpendicular to the blade. Turn the workpiece upside down and cut it in half, being sure to cut with the grain.

Lock the fence ⅜" from the blade and slice the bottom off both halves of the bowl. Glue the two bottom pieces back together along the cut line, being careful to align the surfaces.

Tilt the table again and cut the inside out of the bowl. Try to keep the inside cut parallel to the outside cut.

One of the trickiest parts of making band-sawn bowls is gluing the halves together again. Put glue on the mating edges, then stretch masking tape across the joints to serve as a clamp. I've also had luck using rubber bands as gentle clamps.

Sanding the inside of the bowl can be done by hand, but it takes a long time. For quicker results, use a spindle sander. Also sand the bottom. Finally, place the bowl upside down on your bench and glue the bottom in place, using heavy objects as clamps.

more cutting in three dimensions

As you get more familiar with the idea of cutting in three dimensions, you may surprise yourself with what you can come up with. The sequence of photos on these pages illustrates how to cut a delicate ornament from a chunk of wood simply by making a series of repetitive cuts, applying a little strategic glue, and then making a few more cuts.

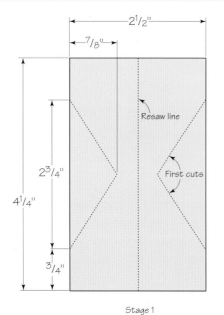

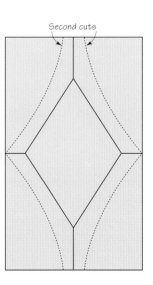

Stage 1   Stage 2

Start by cutting the blank to whatever size you choose and making a pattern for the first cuts. I like to use cardboard for patterns such as this — the kind of cardboard used as a backer for a pad of paper or (as luck would have it) a band saw blade box. Trace the pattern on two adjacent sides of the blank.

Cut along the layout lines on one side of the blank. Save the cutoffs. The more precise you can be with both the layout and the cutting, the better your chances of turning out a truly exquisite little jewel.

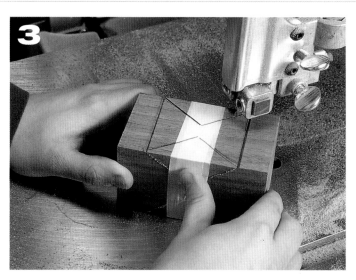

3

Tape the cutoffs back in place to provide support as you cut along the layout lines on the second side. Don't hesitate to add more tape should the pieces start to feel loose.

4

When you are finished with the first round of cuts, your piece will look something like this. Now is the time to sand away the saw marks, as they will be less accessible after the piece is turned in-side out.

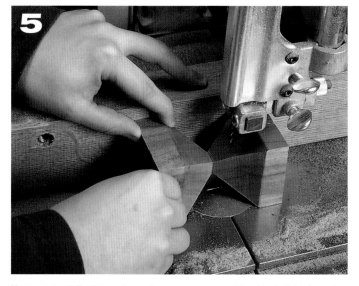

5

Measure carefully, then set up a fence so you can cut the blank right down the middle, dividing it precisely into quadrants.

6

Turn each of the four pieces so its outside is now its inside. Glue the pieces back together in this orientation. It pays to have a lot of clamps for such a glue-up; however, I have made similar glues-ups using tightly stretched rubber bands and masking tape in lieu of clamps.

7

After the glue dries, lay out the cuts on two adjacent sides of the blank again. Again, the more precise you can be with your layouts, the better the final piece will look. Cut along the layout lines on one side of the now hollow blank.

8

Tape the scraps back in place, then cut along the layout lines on the second side of the piece.

9

When you are done cutting, peel away any excess scrap and tape to reveal the finished ornament. As an added touch, you could turn a little bead or bangle to hang inside the hollow form.

cutting cabriole legs

Few forms are more synonymous with fine furniture than the graceful cyma curve of the cabriole leg. While these curvilinear legs are most commonly associated with the furniture styles of the 18th century (namely Queen Anne, Chippendale, and some assorted French ones that I can never keep straight), they have also seen use in some more recent genres, such as Art Nouveau. Regardless of what period you are trying to reproduce, all cabriole legs start out with a series of band saw cuts.

Begin by making a template from a piece of ¼" material. Here, I'm using a piece of plywood that has been painted a light gray color. Take your time laying out the curves and then cutting out the template on the band saw. Sand and smooth the template as well as you can. A good layout goes a long way toward making your work less troublesome.

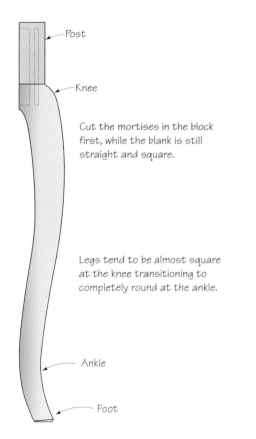

Post

Knee

Cut the mortises in the block first, while the blank is still straight and square.

Legs tend to be almost square at the knee transitioning to completely round at the ankle.

Ankle

Foot

Trace the shape of the template on one side of the leg blank. If you have enough material to be choosy, try to arrange the grain on the blank so the growth rings run diagonally across the piece from the inside corner to the outside corner.

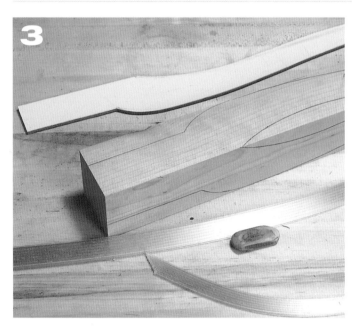

Trace the template on an adjacent side of the leg. Be sure the two layouts come together along the inside corner of the post as shown.

Cut the mortises in the top of the leg while the blank is still straight and square. Once the mortises are cut, cut along the first set of layout lines. Be sure to save the cutoffs; you'll need them.

Tape the cutoffs from the first cuts back in place. These will serve as support for the leg as you make the second series of cuts. Should the cutoff start to loosen as you cut through the tape, don't hesitate to add more tape to hold everything in place.

Clamping a Clamp

Holding on to a cabriole leg as you shape it can be awkward at best. The method I like is to grip the leg with a pipe clamp. Then I can grab the clamp in the front vise on my bench. The toughest part about this setup is remembering to loosen the clamp, not the vise, when I need to reposition the leg.

When you finish cutting, peel the scraps away to reveal the leg. Hold the leg securely and begin to round over the hard edges. The real secret to making a good-looking leg is in making the transition from square at the base of the post to completely round at the ankle. Spokeshaves, scrapers and files are all fair game when it comes to refining the shape of your leg.

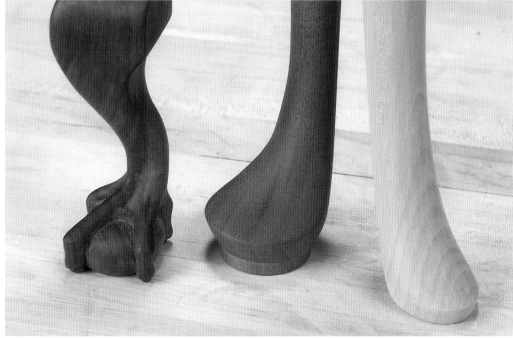

Different styles of cabriole legs are often distinguished by the foot at the bottom. If you have a lathe, you can turn this part of the leg (center). Some of the higher-styled legs in-volved elaborate carvings such as this ball-and-claw foot (left). For a simpler appearance, you can shape the feet directly with your hand tools (right).

maintenance and tune-up

AS MACHINES GO, BAND SAWS ARE not all that complicated. Anything made from an assembly of individual parts, however, has to have those parts in the right relationship to each other in order for the whole thing to work right. This includes making adjustments to the major parts of the machine, such as getting the wheels aligned; as well as setting up the smaller parts, such as the blade guides, so the saw gives you accurate, predictable results. While the specific manner in which you make the adjustments varies from manufacturer to manufacturer, this chapter, used in conjunction with your owner's manual, will give you a good overview of the basics. I think you'll be surprised at how much a few simple adjustments can improve the performance of your saw.

basic alignment

When you first set up your saw, and then once or twice a year thereafter, you should check to make sure the wheels are aligned with each other. This will allow the blade to run true, and it will maximize the amount of power transferred to the cut. Make this adjustment with a blade in place and under full tension. It is best to install the widest blade you normally use on the saw. Having the blade under tension puts all the parts of the saw in the positions they're in when the saw is in use, so you get the most accurate picture of how things are actually aligned.

Tip the table out of the way. Open the doors and hold a long straightedge against the wheels. If they are aligned, the straight-edge will touch each wheel in two places along the rim.

If the wheels are not aligned, hold the straightedge so it touches one of the wheels in two places around its rim. Measure the distance between the straight-edge and the other wheel. This is the amount you need to move that wheel.

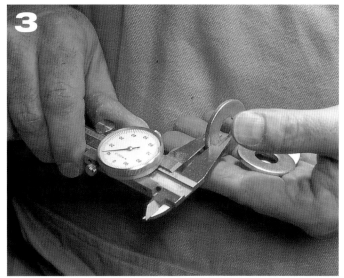

Remove the misaligned wheel and slip enough washers on the axle to move the wheel out the necessary amount. Note, hardware store washers vary somewhat in thickness, so you can probably find a combination of them that will stack up to the right dimension. If not, shim kits are available, or you can snip your own from a soda can.

selecting blades

While not technically an adjustment, selecting the right blade for the job at hand makes a tremendous difference in how well your saw will perform. In all likelihood, the blade that came with your machine will not produce the quality of cut needed for fine woodworking. I recommend you keep it coiled on the wall waiting for the day when you need to cut scraps to fit in the trash can or kindling for the fire. In its place, purchase two or three good blades to cover the various kinds of work you are likely to do. As you shop, you'll need to choose from the following options.

Length

Length is a no-brainer. You need to purchase blades that fit your saw.

Width

The width of the blade determines how tight a curve you can make. Narrow blades can make tight turns but tend to wander more when you try to cut straight (particularly in thicker material). The chart on the next page shows approximately what the various width blades are capable of. In general, I try to choose the widest blade that will allow me to make the cut I am after.

Pitch

The pitch of a blade indicates how many teeth there are per inch (TPI). For thinner stock, you want a blade that has a finer pitch (more teeth). More teeth also means the cut will be smoother, but you won't be able to feed the stock as quickly. For thicker stock, fewer teeth are usually better.

So, if you cut mostly ¾" stock, choose a blade that has 8 to 14 TPI. But if your work deals more with material that is thicker than 1", go with blades that have a courser pitch — 3 to 6 TPI. Note, one of the latest innovations in blade design is blades with variable pitch. On these blades, the tooth count varies. This uneven spacing helps reduce vibration by eliminating the harmonic resonance that can develop in blades with regularly spaced teeth.

Tooth Form

Three types of teeth are commonly available on band saw blades: regular, skip and hook. Blades with finer pitches tend to have regular teeth. They perform well in all materials, though are not good for resawing; (the gullets between the teeth clog with sawdust on thick cuts, greatly reducing the feed rate as well as not cutting well. Skip tooth blades have similar teeth to regular blades, just not as many of them. They tend to cut faster but leave a rougher surface. Hook tooth blades usually have a pitch similar to skip tooth blades. They cut aggressively and are well suited to cutting very hard, dense woods. Their gullets are large and round, which keeps them from clogging. This feature makes a hook tooth blade desirable for resawing. The drawback to a hook tooth blade is that it requires more power than a comparable skip tooth blade.

Thickness

If you have a larger saw (18"+), you can purchase blades made from thicker steel. Thicker blades are stiffer and therefore will cut straighter — an advantage when resawing. They are also more prone to fatigue (which is why they are not made for saws with smaller wheels). Thicker blades also make a wider kerf than thinner blades, thus requiring more power to cut and wasting more wood in the process. Note, some blades made especially for resawing are actually made from thinner-than-average steel. These require less power and less waste. The trade-off is a certain loss of stiffness — which is often worth it.

Material

Most basic band saw blades are made from carbon steel, the main advantage of which is its low cost. If you spend a little more money, you can get blades made from different steel alloys. These often have teeth that are significantly harder than the rest of the blade. So the part that has to flex around the wheels is nice and springy, while the part that has to cut is good and hard. Bimetal blades actually combine two steel alloys with these characteristics. Other manufacturers rely on precision metallurgy to obtain the same result. Carbide-tipped blades are also becoming more readily available. These are significantly more expensive than any of the steel blades but last a lot longer. They do a tremendous job of resawing and, as far as I have experienced, don't tend to drift or lead at all.

Recommendations

So, what do you do with all that information? Basically, try different blades and see what works for you. I like to keep a $\frac{1}{4}$" 4 or 6 TPI skip tooth blade on my saw for general-purpose cutting. I find this blade configuration allows me to make most of the cuts I want to make without having to change blades. As I was putting this book together, Highland Hardware was kind enough to send me one of their $\frac{1}{2}$" Wood Slicer blades. This is an awesome blade for more demanding applications. It yields impressive results when resawing, and I also use it for precision joinery. I also keep both a $\frac{1}{8}$" and a $\frac{1}{16}$" blade on hand for detail work.

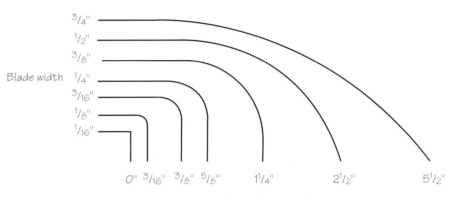

Approximate Blade Capabilities

Blade width: $\frac{3}{4}$" $\frac{1}{2}$" $\frac{3}{8}$" $\frac{1}{4}$" $\frac{3}{16}$" $\frac{1}{8}$" $\frac{1}{16}$"

Approximate radius: 0" $\frac{3}{16}$" $\frac{3}{8}$" $\frac{5}{8}$" $1\frac{1}{4}$" $2\frac{1}{2}$" $5\frac{1}{2}$"

Blade Tune-Up

You can tune up your saw blades by rounding and polishing the back edges. Do this by holding a sharpening stone (I use a cheap Carborundum oilstone) against the blade as it is moving. Be sure to clean the saw thoroughly first to keep any sparks that might occur away from any accumulated sawdust. Rest the stone on a paper tool to avoid scratching the table. Don't push hard on the stone, as you might push the blade out of line. With very narrow blades, you can use a push stick to help keep the blade in place.

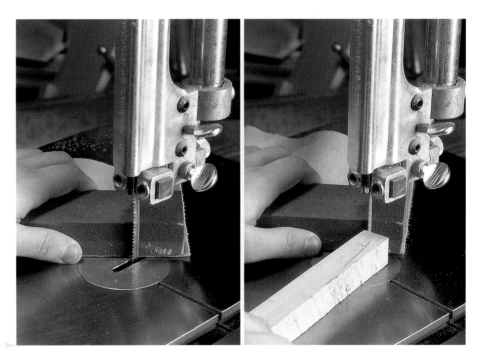

blade tension

Another critical factor in getting your saw to perform at its best is getting the blade tension set right. Blade tension is what keeps the blade from deflecting in the cut, and the cut itself going straight. Older saws use a crank to move the upper wheel and tension the blade. Newer models have a lever that accomplishes the same thing. With both systems, what actually supplies blade tension is a spring. Compressing the spring adds tension to the blade. The spring also serves as a shock absorber and buffer to keep the tension of the blade even.

The lever systems are nice, because they make applying tension a breeze. They have an added advantage in that they also allow you to release the tension immediately. It's a good idea to release the tension at the end of the day to take the stress off the bearings, wheels and other moving parts of the saw. You can get an aftermarket kit that adds this capability to most 14" saws.

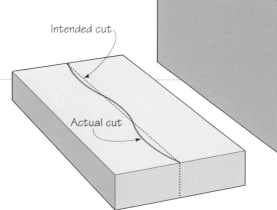

Intended cut

Actual cut

The blade may actually bend within the wood, producing a barrel-shaped cut.

Newer saws have a lever that sets the tension. To use it, you simply pull on the lever until the notch on the hub goes past the lock. If this doesn't provide adequate tension, you can fine-tune the setting with a nut under the spring.

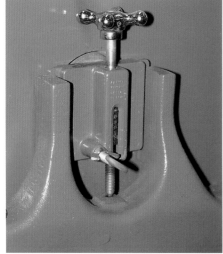

Until recently, most saws used some sort of crank to adjust blade tension. To set the tension, you turn the crank until a mark on the spring aligns with a mark on its housing that indicates the blade width.

Super Spring

Over time, the tension spring on a band saw will become fatigued from the constant compression. Once this happens it will no longer be able to supply the necessary tension to the blade. Iturra Design sells a heavy-duty replacement spring for 14" saws that will give new life to your old saw.

Some controversy exists as to what is the "ideal" tension for a band saw blade. There is also controversy as to how to tell when your blade is properly tensioned. The indicators built into most saws are notoriously inaccurate, which makes it tough to know exactly what you are doing as you crank on the tension adjustment knob. You can also toss into this mix the fact that some blade manufacturers recommend blade tensions, such as 30,000 pounds per square inch (psi), that cannot be achieved on a 14" band saw; the saw just isn't made to apply that much pressure. So how do you know what to do?

Here are some general guidelines to help you answer that question:

• First, realize that both undertensioning and overtensioning a blade can cause trouble. Undertensioned blades don't cut well, and overtensioning can damage your machine.

• Most blades will perform well with a tension between 10,000 and 15,000 psi.

• Determining exactly how much tension your blade is under requires a tension gauge.

• Experiment with your equipment. If you are not satisfied with the results you are getting, try changing the tension. Keep notes as to what works and what doesn't.

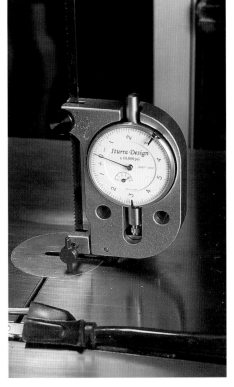

If you use your saw for a lot of demanding applications — resawing thin veneers, cutting precise joinery, etc. — a tension gauge is a worthwhile investment. To use one, clamp it on the blade, then apply tension. The gauge measures how much the blade stretches under load. Conversely, you can attach the gauge to a tensioned blade and then release the tension. The gauge will then register how much the blade "relaxed."

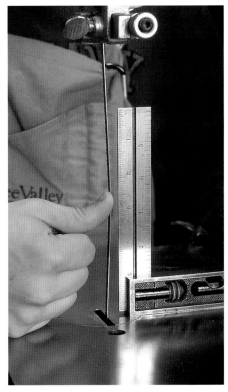

A less technical (and less precise) method of checking blade tension is to raise the blade guard and apply pressure to the side of the blade. Try to determine how much pressure it takes to deflect the blade ¼". If the blade seems to cut well at this tension, try to remember how much pressure you had to apply to the blade.

setting the blade guides

Along with setting the blade tension, the other adjustment you'll make a lot is setting the blade guides. Each time you change blades, you'll need to reset the guides in relationship to the new blade. This usually requires a hex wrench to tighten and loosen the set screws and spacer to get the gap between the guides and the blade right.

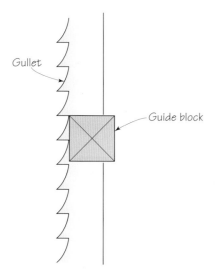

Gullet

Guide block

The blade guides need to be set close to the blade to provide good support but not so close that they are in constant contact. For general use, I find the thickness of a dollar bill provides just the right amount of clearance. Fold the bill around the blade and snug the guide blocks up to it. After tightening the set screws, pull the dollar away, leaving the blocks set perfectly.

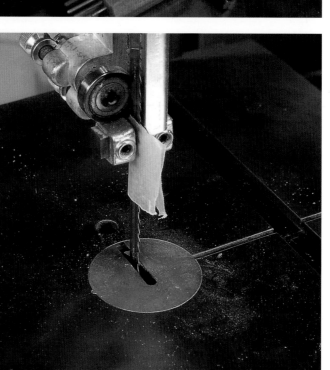

For extremely precise work, I like to have the Guide blocks set a little closer than a dollar allows. Instead I use a piece of 20 lb. bond paper (basic copier fodder). It is slightly thinner than currency, and therefore leaves the guides slightly closer to the blade.

Aftermarket Blade Guides

The steel blade guides that come as standard equipment with most band saws do an adequate job of supporting the blade and keeping it from twisting under most circumstances. But when you start to push the limits of what your saw can do, you find that the steel guides do have limitations.

One of the main arguments against steel guides is that they generate heat and thus shorten blade life. This is an arguable point; some say any heat generated is easily dissipated as the blade runs. I don't have any way of really measuring this, so I can't say one way or the other. But the advantages that some of the aftermarket guides offer make them worth considering.

When you set steel guides, you leave a little space in between them and the blade so they don't rub all the time. This tiny amount of space gives the blade a little room to wander. Ball-bearing guides can be adjusted so they are in contact with the blade at all times and so eliminate that little bit of slop. Several companies make ball-bearing systems. I like Iturra Design's Bandrollers because they are a direct replacement for the steel guides on my Delta saw. This way I can still use the guide controls that are built into the saw.

While ball-bearing guides are an improvement over the regular steel guides, they are not perfect. If you cut a lot of resinous or gummy woods, such as pine or some of the exotics, you'll find the bearings get gummed up with sticky dust fairly quickly. Spaceage Ceramic Guideblocks has developed a ceramic guide block that works well in this situation. The ceramic blocks are incredibly hard and long-wearing. They are so hard, in fact, they are guaranteed for life. They also dissipate heat well. You can set them so they scrape off any accumulated gunk while still keeping the blade on the straight and narrow.

A third type of guide is made from a graphite-impregnated composite. These guides (called Cool Blocks by their inventor, Mark Duginske) are relatively soft and are quite blade friendly. In fact, if you run ⅛" or ¹⁄₁₆" blades, you can sandwich the blade in between a set of Cool Blocks with the teeth totally enclosed within the block. As the saw runs, the blade will cut a notch for itself in the guides. This setup provides great support for the blade, even when backing out of a cut. Because they are graphite impregnated, Cool Blocks actually lubricate the blade slightly as the band saw runs, which makes for a very cool-running machine.

The backup bearing provides support for the blade as the workpiece pushes the blade backward. When the blade is not cutting, there should be a little space between it and the bearing. Here, I use the same dollar (or a five if I'm feeling flush) folded in half to set the clearance.

Iturra Design sells a kit that it calls System Three. It includes three complete sets of blade guides. For woodworkers interested in getting the peak performance from their saws, switching between these guides will give you optimal performance in many different situations. At the top are ball-bearing guides, in the center are ceramic guides, and to the right are graphite-impregnated composite guides. The kit also includes excellent quality backup bearings so you can replace the originals on your saw when they fail.

other tune-ups

Here are a few other tricks you can try to improve your band saw's performance as well as its versatility in your shop.

If your saw seems underpowered or suffers from excessive vibration, try switching to a segmented drive belt. These multipiece belts transfer power from the motor to the lower wheel more smoothly and efficiently than a regular V-belt does.

Band saws throw a lot of fine dust into the air. Your nose and lungs will thank you if you try to contain the mess before it becomes airborne. Newer saws often have built-in dust ports. However, if you have an older model, you may have to be creative. On several old saws I've used, I've had good luck cutting a hole in the back of the lower housing and attaching a pipe flange to which I could attach a vacuum hose.

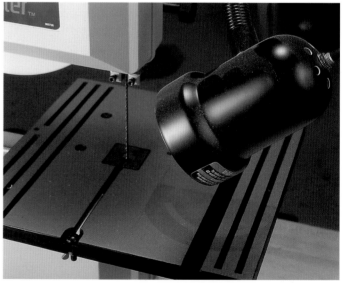

Another feature many manufacturers now offer is a work light. With their upper wheel jutting up into the air, band saws cast odd shadows onto the work. A work light can be just the ticket to let you really see what is going on. Use a heavy-duty bulb such as the ones sold for use in garage door openers. Their filaments are tougher and stand up to the vibrations the saw is likely to inflict.

If your band saw doesn't come equipped with a work light, don't feel you have to buy a special one for your saw. I've used this old task light successfully on my big band saw for years. It's attached to a post behind the saw and can easily swing into position. And because my drill press is near the band saw, the light does double duty as I drill.

If you are cramped for space, a mobile base allows you to roll your saw out when you need it, then stash it out of the way when you are done. This base is nice because the casters flip up and down via a lever I can operate with my foot.

Friends of mine have a different approach to machine mobility. They make timber frames for houses in their shop and often have to cut pieces that are too big to move easily. Instead, they have their 14" band saw on a simple plywood dolly like this one with four pivoting casters. This allows them to move the saw through the cut. I've watched them do this, and it looks a lot like they are waltzing with the saw.

band sawn boxes

MAKING BOXES WITH A BAND SAW opens up a whole new world of design possibilities. With most wooden boxes, you have to work around the constraints of the material and joinery used to put the pieces together. Not so with a band sawn box. Here, the size and shape of the box are pretty much limited only by your imagination and the capacity of your saw.

Regardless of the shape and size of your box, the process of making a band-sawn box is pretty much the same. You make a series of cuts, getting rid of the material you don't want, and then you glue back together the various parts you want to keep. It is important to plan ahead and make the cuts in the right order so you don't cut away parts of the blank you'll need for support later.

In most cases, you'll start by slicing away the top and bottom of the box. These can be straight cuts, but they don't have to be. Next, you'll hollow out the box body. Then you can reunite the hollow box body with the bottom you cut away earlier. With careful clamping and good sanding, the cut/glue lines will practically disappear.

Two boxes are presented here. The first is a straightforward box that will serve as an excellent introduction to the joys of making containers on the band saw. The second is a simple jewelry case made with three drawers.

simple box

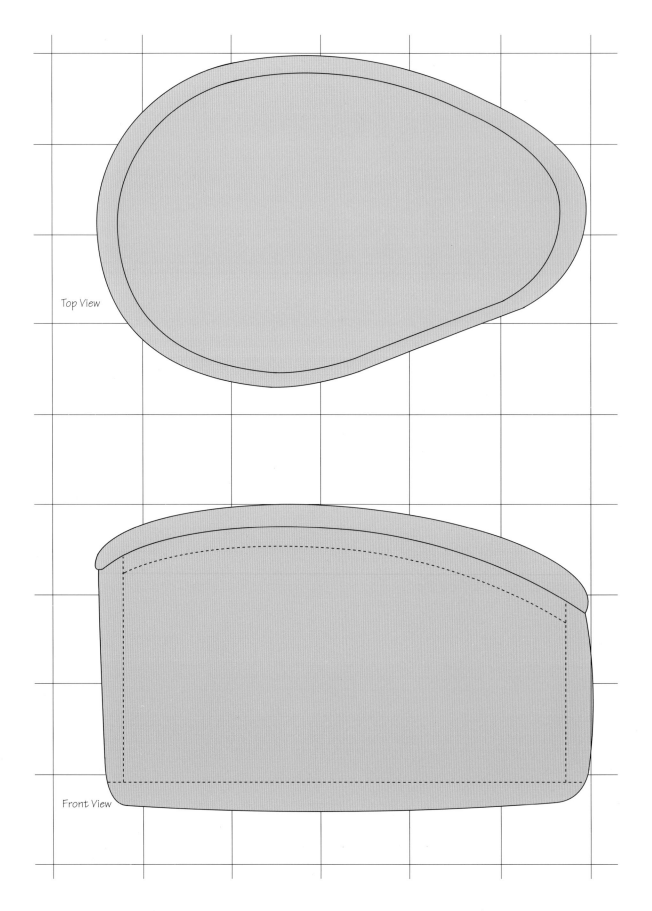

Top View

Front View

Start by cutting a ¼" slice off the blank to form the bottom.

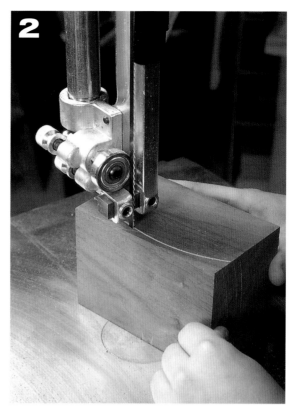

Lay out the contour of the box's top on the side of the piece. Cut along this line.

Lay out the cut that will separate the lid from the rest of the box. This line could be parallel to the cut you just made, but it doesn't have to be. Make the cut.

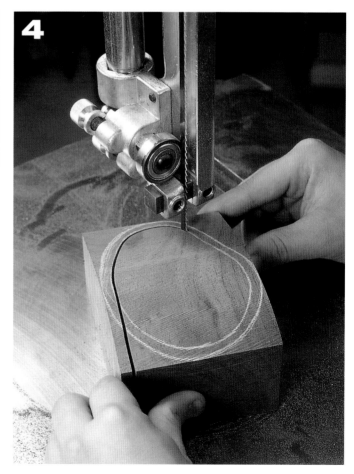

Lay out the cut that will hollow out the box. Start cutting with the grain. Cut around the inside of the box, then carefully back the blade out through the entry slot.

Hold the center section in place on the top. Trace around the inside of the box to mark its location on the underside of the top.

Cut a thin (1/8" +/-) slice off the plug left over from hollowing out the box. This slice should follow the contour of the cut you made in step 2.

Gently sand the edges of the slice you just cut. Glue this piece to the underside of the top, aligning it with the traced outline of the box interior.

Work glue into the entry slot in the center section. Gently clamp the slot closed. Glue and clamp the bottom in place as well.

9

Tape the lid in place. Lay out the outside shape of the box, then cut the box to shape.

10

Sand the outside of the box to remove all the saw marks and polish the wood. Apply several coats of your favorite finish.

11

Paint the inside of the box. You can also paint the underside of the lid if you'd like.

12

While the paint is still wet, dump in a quantity of flocking and shake it around to coat all the wet surfaces. Dump out the excess. Allow the paint to dry and you're done.

▨ *box with drawers*

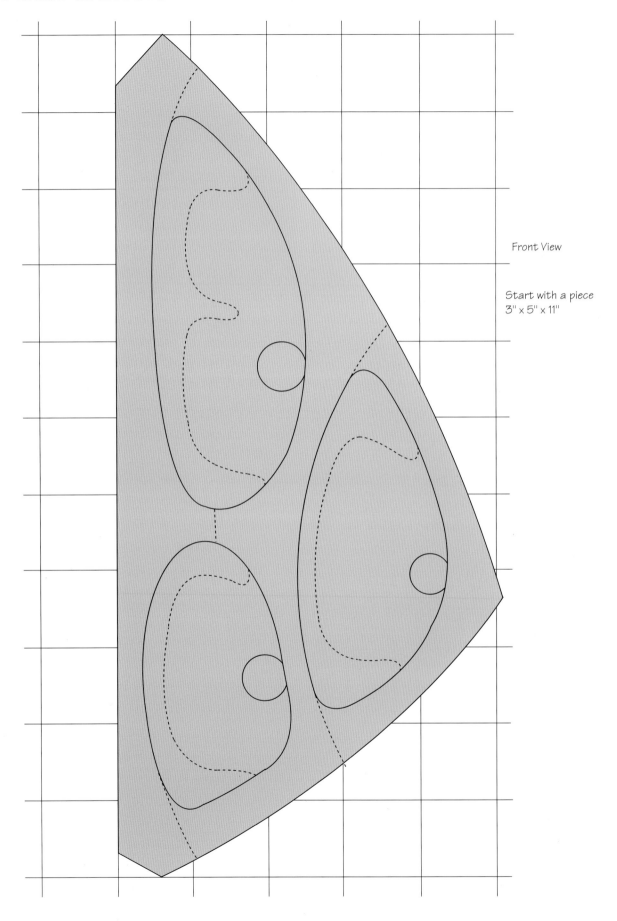

Front View

Start with a piece
3" x 5" x 11"

1

Unless you're lucky enough to have a thick chunk of wood available, you'll need to glue two or more pieces to make up the required thickness. Flatten the pieces, then spread glue on the mating surfaces and clamp everything together.

2

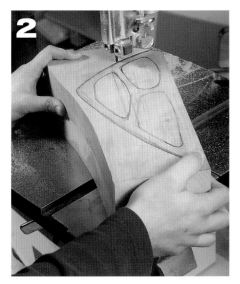

Draw the outline of the box on your workpiece. Cut the piece to shape.

3

Set up a fence and cut a ¼" slice off the back side of the workpiece to form the back.

4

Lay out the outlines of the drawers on the front face of the workpiece. Cut out the left-hand bottom drawer first, starting the cut as shown.

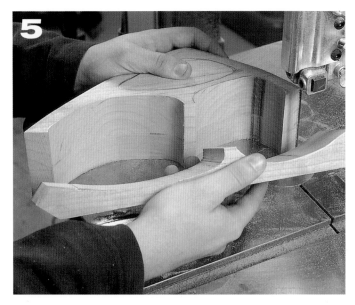

5

Cut across the bottom of the divider to gain access to the right-hand drawer. Cut around the drawer, then out the side of the workpiece as shown. Repeat the process for the upper drawer, cutting in from one side and out the other.

6

Apply glue to the mating surfaces and clamp the three pieces of the case back together. Be careful to keep the pieces perfectly in line along the back.

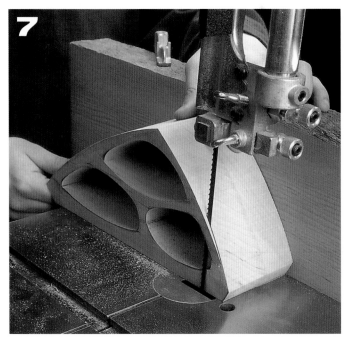

7

Tip the table on your band saw over a few degrees and bevel the front of the case. You can make this cut along a slight arc to add a little more dimension to the design if you desire.

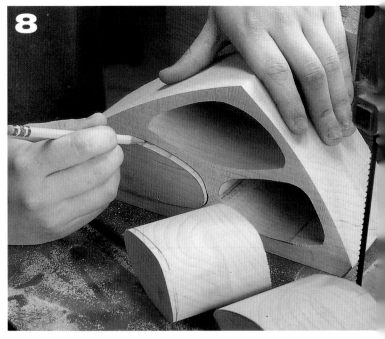

8

Slip the drawer blanks into their respective holes. Trace the contour of the case front onto the blanks, leaving $1/8$" or so extra to allow for the kerfs you will make when you hollow out the drawers.

9

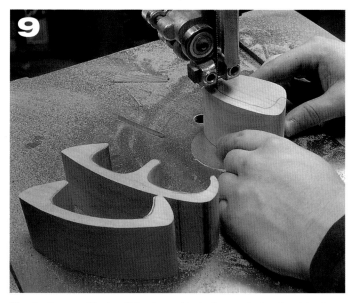

Slice the fronts and backs off the drawer blanks. Lay out the interior of the drawers, leaving the walls and bottom about $1/4$"-thick. Feel free to leave dividers in the drawers if you would like. Cut along the lines to hollow the drawers.

10

With the extra material on the drawer fronts, you can sculpt integral handles into them. Or you can cut away the excess to make the fronts flush with the rest of the case. If you intend to make the fronts flush, cut finger holes into their top edges as shown.

11

If you want the fronts flush with the case, tip the table on your saw to the necessary angle. Fasten the front to a longer piece of scrap with double-sided tape for stability. Cut all the fronts to the desired contour.

12

Sand all the surfaces of the box. You may find using an inflatable drum sander takes away a lot of the hassle associated with this process. Use sandpaper to tune up the fit of the drawers in the case; you're looking for an even gap all around the front when the drawer is closed. Finish the piece with your favorite wood finish. When dry, paint and flock the insides of the drawers.

dvd cabinet

IN THE PAST FEW YEARS, THE DVD has become the medium of choice for home video. And now, as DVD recorders become more affordable, these devices are supplanting videotapes, slide carousels and even photo albums as the repository for the family archives. I have to admit I'm a big fan of these shimmering, silver discs. What I don't like, however, is the way DVD cases look. They're really too narrow to look good on a typical bookcase. And the garish colors that often adorn the covers are just not what I want to have on display. So, after putting up with a growing pile of DVDs without any good way of storing them, I designed this wall-hung cabinet as a solution to the problem.

The cabinet features bookmatched panels in its doors. I resawed the panels from a highly figured board and glued it to some less figured pieces of the same species. This let me get a little more mileage from the figured material while creating a nice symmetrical look for the cabinet itself. The rest of the construction is straightforward. The case is assembled with tongue-and-groove joints reinforced with screws. Contrasting plugs cover the screw heads. If you feel ambitious, you could dovetail the corners, although the added strength is not needed. A face frame with a shaped lower rail and a top with tapered edges complete the unit.

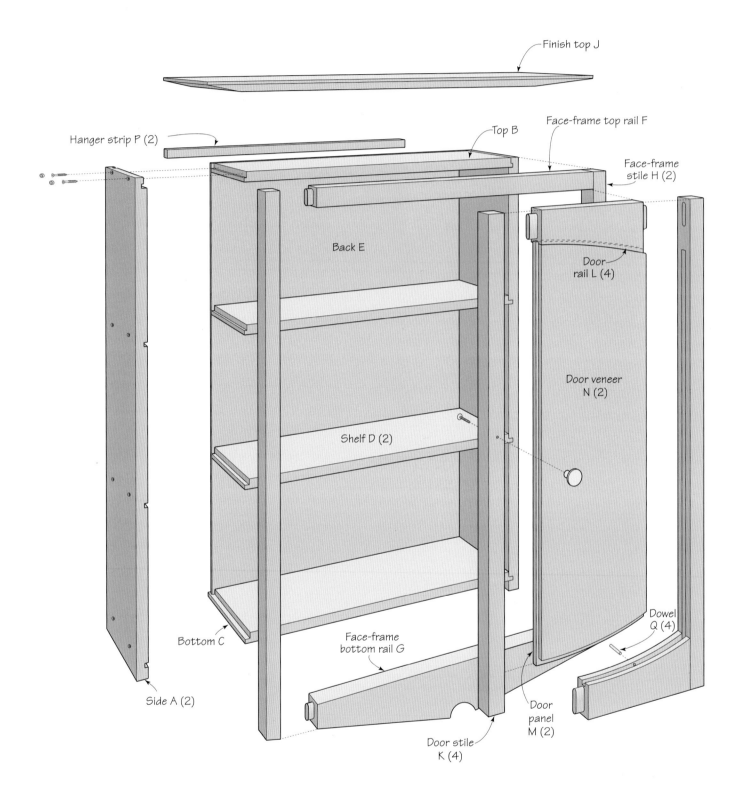

Finish top J

Hanger strip P (2)

Top B

Face-frame top rail F

Face-frame stile H (2)

Back E

Door rail L (4)

Door veneer N (2)

Shelf D (2)

Bottom C

Face-frame bottom rail G

Dowel Q (4)

Side A (2)

Door panel M (2)

Door stile K (4)

REFERENCE	QUANTITY	PART	STOCK	THICKNESS	(mm)	WIDTH	(mm)	LENGTH	(mm)
A	2	sides	hardwood	3/4	(19)	7	(178)	31 1/2	(800)
B	1	top	hardwood	3/4	(19)	6 1/4	(159)	21 3/4	(553)
C	1	bottom	hardwood	3/4	(19)	7	(178)	21 3/4	(553)
D	2	shelves	hardwood	3/4	(19)	6 1/4	(159)	21 3/4	(553)
E	1	back	hardwood plywood	1/4	(6)	21 3/4	(553)	31 1/8	(791)
F	1	face-frame top rail	hardwood	1	(25)	1 1/4	(32)	20	(508)
G	1	face-frame bottom rail	hardwood	1	(25)	3 1/8	(79)	20	(508)
H	2	face-frame stiles	hardwood	1	(25)	1 1/4	(32)	31 3/4	(807)
J	1	finish top	hardwood	1	(25)	10	(254)	30	(762)
K	4	door stiles	hardwood	1	(25)	1 3/8	(35)	28 3/4	(730)
L	4	door rails	hardwood	1	(25)	3 3/4	(95)	7 1/4	(184)
M	2	door panels	hardwood	3/4	(19)	7 3/4	(197)	25 3/4	(654)
N	2	door veneer	figured hardwood	1/8	(3)	7 3/4	(197)	25 3/4	(654)
P	2	hanger strips	hardwood	1/2	(13)	1	(25)	21	(533)
Q	4	dowels	hardwood	1/8 dia.	(3)			1/2	(13)

MATERIALS & SUPPLIES

21 No. 8 x 1 5/8 (41mm) screws

16 3/8" (10mm) plugs

4 1 1/2"-wide x 2 (38mm-wide x 51mm) brass hinges with screws

2 bullet catches with screws

2 brass knobs

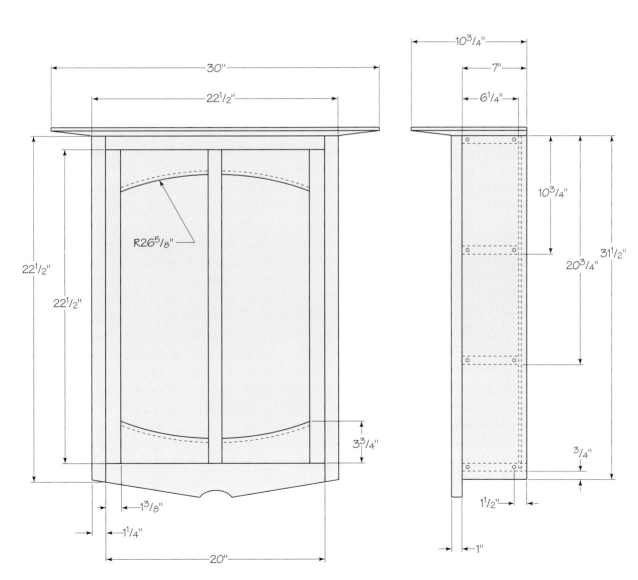

Front View

Side View

Cut the sides, top, bottom and shelves to the sizes listed. Set up a 1/4" dado head on your table saw and cut grooves across the sides for the top, bottom and shelves. The spacing for these grooves is shown in the Side View.

Using the same dado setup, cut a groove for the back in the sides and bottom. This groove should be 1/2" in from the back edges of the pieces.

Increase the width of the dado to $5/8$". Set the fence slightly more than $1/4$" away from the blade. Cut a sample tongue on one of the shelves by running the piece on end along the fence. Check the fit of the tongue in the groove; it should be too thick. Bump the fence over a little and recut. Repeat the process until the tongue fits snugly in the groove. Cut tongues on the shelves, top and bottom.

Lay out the location of the screw holes on the sides. Drill $3/16$" holes through the sides for the screws and $3/8$" holes partway through for the plugs. Set up a fence on your drill press to help keep the holes spaced consistently. Sand all the pieces.

Apply glue to the grooves, then quickly insert the tongues. Make sure the back edges of the top and shelves end up flush with the front edge of the grooves you cut in the sides for the back. Drill pilot holes and screw the pieces together. Slide the back in place to help hold the cabinet square. Plug the screw holes and sand the plugs flush with the sides.

Checking for Square

A great tool for taking diagonal measurements is a folding rule. Try to find one with the extension "swizzle stick" at one end. You can fold one of these rules in such a way that the extension can be pushed right into the corner. When you check the opposite diagonal, the extension should protrude the same amount if the case is square.

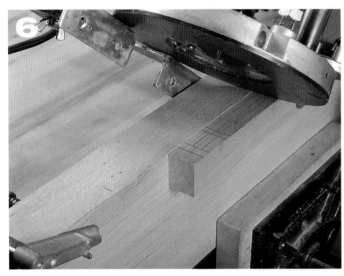

Cut the face-frame rails and stiles to the widths and lengths specified in the materials list. Note, the stiles are slightly long; you'll trim them later. Cut mortises in the stiles with a plunge router. I find it easiest to do this by clamping the pieces to a wider piece of stock to provide a stable base for the router. Refer to the Face-Frame Detail on the next page for the proper placement.

Cut tenons on the ends of the face-frame rails. Make the shoulder cuts on the table saw, then make the cheek cuts on the band saw.

8

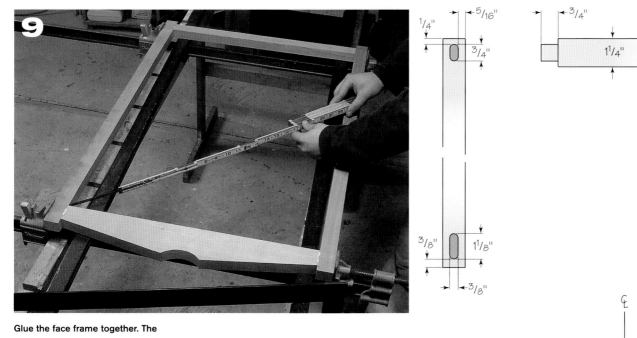

Lay out the shape of the bottom rail as shown in the Face-Frame Detail. Cut the rail to shape on the band saw and sand away the saw marks.

9

Glue the face frame together. The extra length on the stiles provides reinforcement to the joints during glue-up. Use a straightedge to make sure the frame is flat. Also check the diagonal measurements to make sure the frame is square.

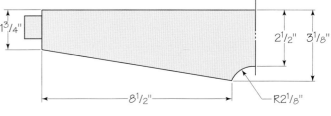

FACE FRAME DETAIL

10

Once the glue dries, trim the ends of the stiles flush with the rails. The cuts at the bottom of the frame should be angled to match the shape of the bottom rail.

11

Glue the face frame to the front of the case. After the glue dries, trim the frame flush with the case with a block plane.

12

Tip the table on your band saw over about 10°. Set up a fence, leaving a 5/16" gap between it and the blade at the table. Bevel the front edge and ends of the finish top by running the piece along the fence. Sand away all the saw marks. Glue the finish top to the case.

13

Cut the door stiles and rails to the sizes listed. Make the mortise-and-tenon joints as you did for the face frame. After you cut the tenons on the rails, lay out the curves, then cut the pieces to shape.

14

Resaw a piece of figured stock to make the veneer for the door panels. Glue the veneers to some lesser pieces to make up the actual panels. Be sure to bookmatch the pieces if you want a symmetrical look to your cabinet.

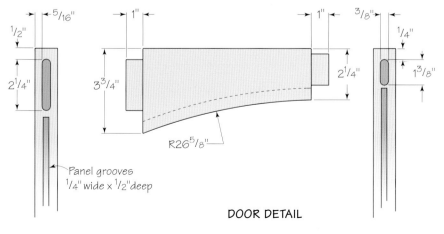

Panel grooves
$1/4$" wide x $1/2$" deep

R26$5/8$"

DOOR DETAIL

15

Cut the grooves for the door panels in the frame pieces with a wing cutter chucked in a table-mounted router. You can use a straight fence with the stiles, stopping the grooves just before they meet the mortises. With the rails, however, you'll need to cut a curved fence to match their radius. Make a cutout in the fence for the cutter as shown. All the grooves should be $3/8"$ deep.

16

Assemble the door frames without glue. Place the frames on top of the panels and trace around their inside edges to mark the panels. Draw a second set of lines $3/8"$ outside of the first set to show where to cut the panels. Cut the panels to shape.

17

Rout a $1/2"$-wide rabbet around the edges of both panels. Adjust the height of the router bit to make the resulting tongue fit in the groove in the door frame pieces.

Glue the door frames together (be sure to remember to put the panels in place, first). When the glue dries, center the panels in the frames and pin them in place with two pieces of $1/8$" dowel, one in the center of the top rail and one in the center of the bottom rail. Drill the holes from the back side of the frame so they won't show.

Bevel one edge of both hanger strips at about a 30° angle. Cut one of the strips to fit along the top edge of the back of the cabinet. Screw the hanger in place. The other hanger strip gets attached to the wall when you are ready to hang the cabinet.

Fit the doors to the opening. Cut matching mortises in the door frames and in the face frame. You can do this all with a chisel, but I find it easier to rout the mortises with the aid of a simple shop-made mortising jig (see "A Router Mortising Jig" in chapter four). Finish the cabinet, then install the hinges, the catches and the rest of the hardware.

console table with shapely legs

WITH ITS CABRIOLE LEGS AND cutout apron, the design of this table is reminiscent of 18th-century furniture. Although I looked at some photographs of period furniture as I drew it, the design is more of an interpretation of Queen Anne and Chippendale style than it is a true reproduction. What it will do, however, is put your band saw skills to the test. In addition to sawing the curvaceous legs and undulating aprons, you'll cut dovetails to assemble the drawer, do some resawing on the drawer front and cut tenons on the aprons. In all, you'll give your band saw a complete workout as well as build a fine piece of furniture.

The table in the photo is made from black walnut with hard maple as a secondary wood (drawer sides and running parts). The legs were cut from pieces that were a full 3" thick. A piece of this heavy stock was also used to make the drawer front. The drawer front's construction is a bit unique in that the piece is resawn so you can cut the dovetails on the band saw. Then, after gluing the two pieces back together, you can cut both the inside and the outside to the proper curvature. In all, I think it is a pretty sneaky way to create a complex-appearing detail.

[PROJECT THREE]

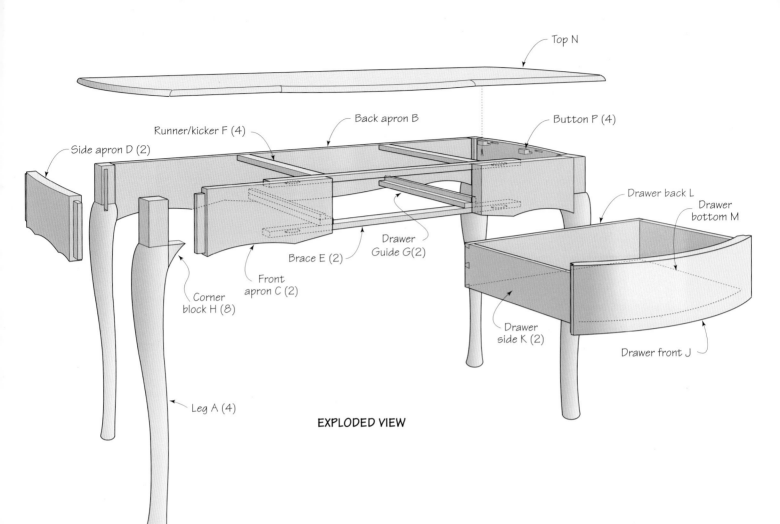

Top N

Back apron B

Button P (4)

Runner/kicker F (4)

Side apron D (2)

Drawer back L

Drawer bottom M

Corner block H (8)

Brace E (2)

Front apron C (2)

Drawer Guide G(2)

Drawer side K (2)

Drawer front J

Leg A (4)

EXPLODED VIEW

REFERENCE	**QUANTITY**	**PART**	**STOCK**	**THICKNESS**	**(mm)**	**WIDTH**	**(mm)**	**LENGTH**	**(mm)**	
A	4	legs	hardwood	3	(76)	3	(76)	27	(686)	
B	1	back apron	hardwood	1	(25)	5$\frac{1}{2}$	(140)	48$\frac{1}{2}$	(1232)	
C	2	front aprons	hardwood	1	(25)	5$\frac{1}{2}$	(140)	14$\frac{1}{4}$	(362)	
D	2	side aprons	hardwood	1$\frac{3}{4}$	(45)	5$\frac{1}{2}$	(140)	15$\frac{1}{8}$	(384)	
E	2	braces	secondary hardwood	$\frac{1}{2}$	(13)	1	(25)	28	(711)	
F	4	runners/kickers	secondary hardwood	$\frac{1}{2}$	(13)	1$\frac{1}{2}$	(38)	13$\frac{15}{16}$	(354)	
G	2	drawer guides	secondary hardwood	$\frac{1}{2}$	(13)	$\frac{1}{2}$	(13)	13$\frac{15}{16}$	(354)	
H	8	corner blocks	hardwood	1$\frac{1}{2}$	(38)	1$\frac{1}{2}$	(38)	1$\frac{1}{2}$	(38)	
J	1	drawer front	hardwood	2$\frac{3}{8}$	(60)	4$\frac{7}{8}$	(124)	17	(432)	
K	2	drawer sides	secondary hardwood	$\frac{1}{2}$	(13)	3$\frac{1}{4}$	(83)	14$\frac{1}{2}$	(368)	
L	1	drawer back	secondary hardwood	$\frac{1}{2}$	(13)	3$\frac{1}{4}$	(83)	16$\frac{1}{4}$	(413)	
M	1	drawer bottom	hardwood plywood	$\frac{1}{4}$	(6)	15$\frac{13}{16}$	(402)	15$\frac{1}{2}$	(394)	
N	1	top	hardwood	1	(25)	20$\frac{1}{2}$	(521)	53$\frac{3}{4}$	(1365)	
P	4	buttons	secondary hardwood	$\frac{3}{4}$	(19)	1$\frac{1}{4}$	(32)	1$\frac{1}{2}$	(38)	

MATERIALS LIST inches (millimeters)

HARDWARE & SUPPLIES

4   No. 8 x 1$\frac{1}{4}$" (32mm) brass roundhead wood screws

1   $\frac{3}{4}$" (19mm) diameter brass knob

1

Start by cutting the mortises in the legs. Then make a template so you can trace the curves on two sides of each of the four legs. Cut the legs to shape. Finish shaping the legs with files, scrapers and sandpaper.

2

Cut tenons on the ends of the front and back aprons to fit the mortises you routed in the legs. The mortises intersect inside the legs, so you'll need to miter the inside corners of the tenons so they can actually seat all the way.

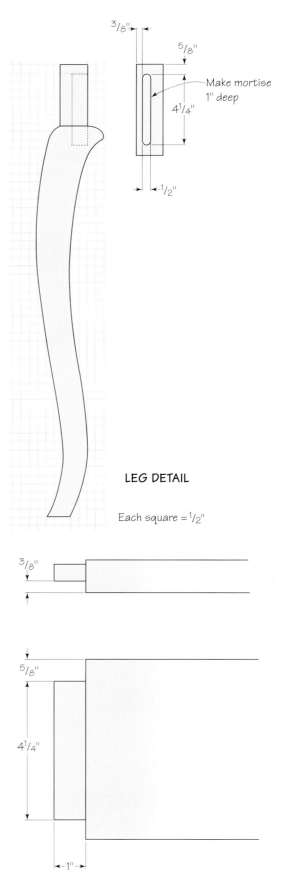

3/8"
5/8"
Make mortise 1" deep
4 1/4"
1/2"

LEG DETAIL

Each square = 1/2"

3/8"

5/8"

4 1/4"

1"

TENON DETAILS

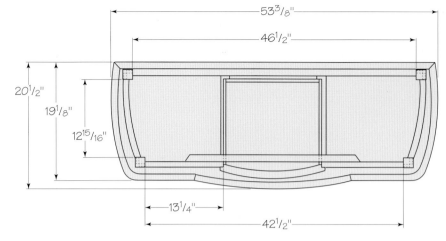

TOP VIEW

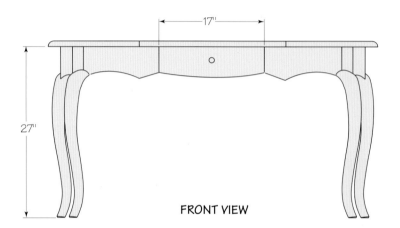

FRONT VIEW

Because the side aprons run at an angle, their tenons are a little tricky to cut. Cut the apron pieces to the listed thickness and width, but leave them slightly long for now. Glue opposing wedges to the front and back of the pieces. After the glue dries, joint one side to make sure the wedges are even. Rip the assembly on the band saw to even out the wedges on the other side.

Cut one end of the wedge assembly square. Then use a stop on the miter gauge fence as you cut the second end. This guarantees both pieces will be the same length. Note, by cutting the pieces with the wedges attached, you'll actually be making bevel cuts on the ends of the aprons.

5

While you have the miter gauge on the saw, make the shoulder cuts for the tenons. Lay out the joints first, then use the fence as a stop to control the length of the tenons.

6

Lay out the curves on the top edges of the side aprons. Make the cuts on the band saw, cutting off the wedges at the same time. Rout slots for the buttons that hold the top in the inside face of the aprons ½" down from their top edges.

7

Dry clamp the table base together. Hold the braces in place in between the two front aprons and mark them to show their position in relationship to the drawer opening.

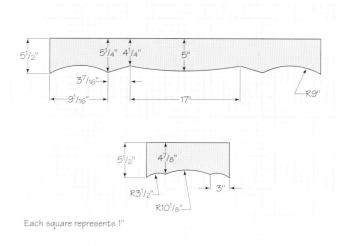

5½"   5¼" 4¼"   5"

3⁷⁄₁₆"

9¹⁄₁₆"   17"   R9"

5½"   4⁷⁄₈"

R3½"   3"

R10¹⁄₈"

Each square represents 1"

APRON DETAIL

8

Glue the braces to the insides of the front aprons. You may find it easier to add biscuit joints in between the pieces to help keep everything aligned. Be sure to align the marks you made on the braces with the ends of the aprons so the drawer opening (and the length of the front apron assembly) is correct.

9

Use a plunge router equipped with an edge guide to mortise the front and back aprons for the drawer runners and kickers. If the router's base isn't big enough to ride on both braces (and is therefore tippy), cut some spacers to fill in underneath. Cut tenons on the ends of the runners and kickers to fit the mortises.

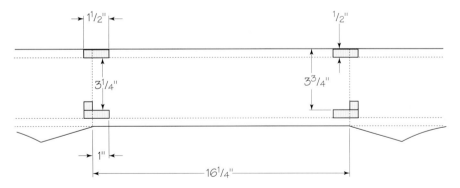

RUNNER & KICKER DETAILS

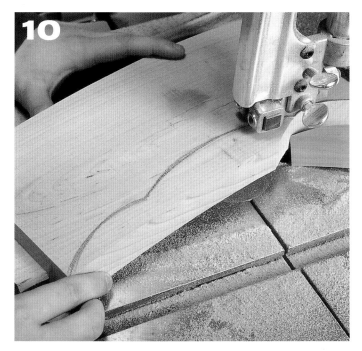

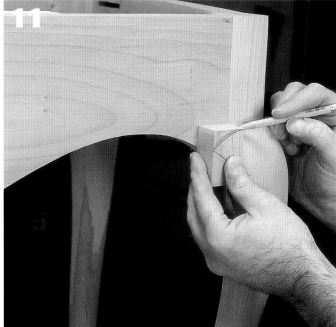

Lay out the curved profiles along the bottoms of the aprons as shown in the Apron Details. Cut the pieces to shape.

Sand all the pieces and glue the table base together. Hold the corner blocks in place and trace the profile of the legs on them. Cut them roughly to shape. File and sand them until they are almost right, then glue them in place. Sand them to final shape when the glue dries. Note, on the sides you may need to cut a flat on the aprons to glue the corner blocks to.

Make an alignment mark across the top edge of the drawer front. This will make it easier to align the pieces when you glue them back together. Resaw a 1/2"-thick slice off the back of the blank. Cut the 1/2" piece to length so it just barely fits in the drawer opening in the front apron. Be sure to remove an equal amount off each end so the drawer front stays centered.

13

Dovetail the corners of the drawer. Note, the half pins on the drawer front are much wider than what you might expect.

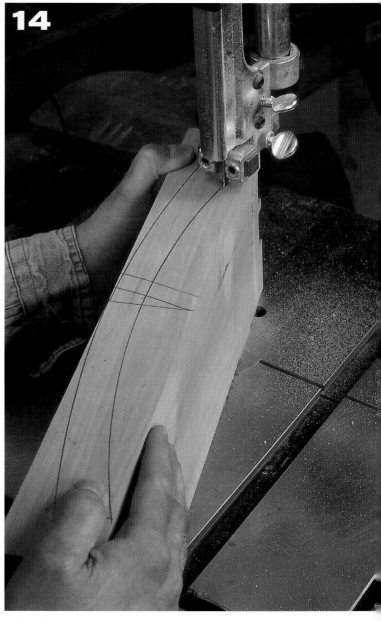

14

Glue the $\frac{1}{2}$" piece back on the rest of the drawer front. Center the piece so the rabbet created at each end is equal. Clean out any glue from inside the dovetails. After the glue dries, lay out the curves on the top edge of the drawer front. Make the cuts, then sand the piece to clean up the saw marks.

DRAWER JOINERY DETAILS

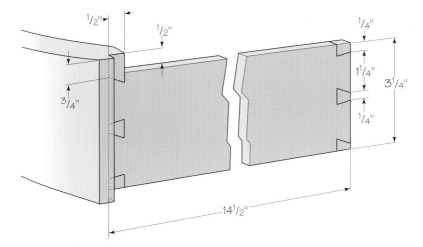

$\frac{1}{2}$" $\frac{1}{2}$" $\frac{3}{4}$" $\frac{1}{4}$" $1\frac{1}{4}$" $3\frac{1}{4}$" $\frac{1}{4}$" $14\frac{1}{2}$"

15

Use a wing cutter in a router table to cut the grooves in the drawer parts to hold the bottom. For the straight pieces, you can use a regular fence to guide the pieces. For the drawer front, you'll need to make a curved fence that matches its curvature. (See step 15 in chapter eight for a similar setup.) Sand and assemble the drawer.

16

Glue up material for the top. Cut the top to shape and smooth the curves. Rout a thumbnail profile all around the edges. Rout grooves in the side aprons. Make buttons with short tongues on one end to fit in the grooves. Turn the top upside down on your bench with the base centered on top of it. Slip the buttons in the grooves and screw them to the top, locking it in place. Finish the table with your favorite wood finish. Note, the bottom of the back apron should be cut to match the front; I ran out of time and had to improvise to get this photo taken.

DRAWER FRONT DETAIL

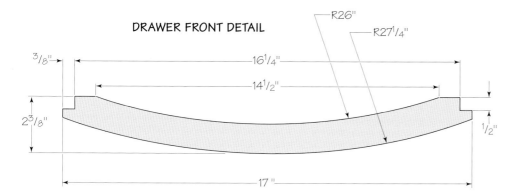

R26"
R27¹/₄"
³/₈"
16¹/₄"
14¹/₂"
2³/₈"
¹/₂"
17"

suppliers

ADAMS & KENNEDY– THE WOOD SOURCE
6178 Mitch Owen Road
P.O. Box 700
Manotick, Ontario, Canada K4M 1A6
613-822-6800
www.wood-source.com
Wood supply

B&Q
B&Q Head Office
Portswood House
1 Hampshire Corporate Park
Chandlers Ford
Eastleigh
Hampshire
SO53 3YX
023 8025 6256
www.diy.com
Tools, paint, wood, electrical, garden

CONSTANTINES WOOD CENTER
1040 East Oakland Park Boulevard
Fort Lauderdale, Florida 33334
800-443-9667
www.constantines.com
Tools, wood, veneers, hardware

DELTA MACHINERY
4825 Highway 45 North
P.O. Box 2468
Jackson, Tennessee 38302-2468
800-223-7278
www.deltawoodworking.com
Woodworking machine tools

FOCUS (DIY) LIMITED
Gawsworth House
Westmere Drive
Crewe
Cheshire
CW1 6XB
0800 436 436
www.focusdiy.co.uk
Tools and home woodworking equipment

HIGHLAND HARDWARE
1045 North Highland Avenue, NE
Atlanta, Georgia 30306
800-241-6748
www.highlandhardware.com
*General woodworking supplies and tools;
Wood Slicer band saw blades*

HOMEBASE LTD.
Beddington House
Railway Approach
Wallington
SM6 0HB
0845 077 8888
www.homebase.co.uk
Tools and home woodworking equipment

THE HOME DEPOT
2455 Paces Ferry Road
Atlanta, Georgia 30339
800-553-3199 (U.S.)
800-668-2266 (Canada)
www.homedepot.com
Tools, paint, wood, electrical, garden

HOUSE OF TOOLS LTD.
100 Mayfield Common Northwest
Edmonton, Alberta, Canada T5P 4B3
800-661-3987
www.houseoftools.com
Woodworking tools and hardware

HOYLE PRODUCTS, INC.
10675 Highway 155
P.O. Box 490
Glennville, California 93226
800-345-1950
www.hoylegrips.com
Acu-Arc ruler, flexible drawing splines

ITURRA DESIGN
4636 Fulton Road
Jacksonville, Florida 32225
888-722-7078
e-mail: kall@comcast.net
Band saw accessories

LANGEVIN & FOREST LTE.
9995 Boulevard Pie XI
Montreal, Quebec, Canada H1Z 3X1
800-889-2060
Tools, wood and books

LEE VALLEY TOOLS
P.O. Box 1780
Ogdensburg, New York 13669
800-871-8158
www.leevalley.com
*General woodworking supplies and tools;
rare earth magnets*

LOWE'S HOME IMPROVEMENT WAREHOUSE
P.O. Box 1111
North Wilkesboro, North Carolina 28656
800-445-6937
www.lowes.com
Tools, paint, wood, electrical, garden

MICRO JIG, INC.
P.O. Box 195607
Winter Springs, Florida 32719
407-696-6695
www.microjig.com
Jigs and safety devices

ROCKLER WOODWORKING AND HARDWARE
4365 Willow Drive
Medina, Minnesota 55340
800-279-4441
www.rockler.com
Woodworking tools and hardware

RYOBI TECHNOLOGIES, INC.
1428 Pearman Dairy Road
Anderson, South Carolina 29625
800-323-4615
www.ryobitools.com
Woodworking power tools

WINDY RIDGE WOODWORKS
6751 Hollenbach Road
New Tripoli, Pennsylvania 18066
610-767-4515
e-mail: ksburton@fast.net
Custom woodworking, freelance writing, woodworking workshops

WOLFCRAFT NORTH AMERICA
333 Swift Road
Addison, Illinois 60101
630-773-4777
www.wolfcraft.com
Woodworking hardware and accessories

WOODCRAFT
P.O. Box 1686
Parkersburg, West Virginia 26102
800-225-1153
www.woodcraft.com
General woodworking supplies and tools

WOODWORKER'S SUPPLY
1108 North Glenn Road
Casper, Wyoming 82601
800-645-9292
www.woodworker.com
Woodworking tools and accessories; finishing supplies; books and plans

index